UNDEFEATED
Broken into Purpose

Khalilah Johnson

Edited by Debora M. Ricks

Cover by Awesome Ministry

Photography by Leslie Arnelle

To book Khalilah Johnson for speaking engagements visit:

undefeatabeministries.com

Undefeatable Ministries Publishing

ISBN-13: 978-0996983006

ISBN-10: 0996983007

BISAC: Family & Relationships / Dysfunctional Families

To protect the privacy of certain individuals the names and
identifying details have been changed.

Table of Contents

I Dedicate Undefeated:

To my beautiful Mother, who has endured great pain but her smile can light up a room. Your prayers have sustained us. You taught me the power of prayer. You are Undefeated!

To my Grandmother who has shown resilience, strength and wisdom. Your prayers for God to save me, no matter what it takes, are being answered.

To my beautiful and brilliant daughter Kaira, your gifts and talents will one day impact this world. You are great, and come from a lineage of overcomers with immeasurable possibilities, and undiscovered potential. Never dim your light, shine bright and always trust God.

INTRODUCTION

By the Grace of God, I have defeated the odds through surrender, forgiveness and obedience. Every time I tell my story, I receive healing, restoration, and deliverance. Through my process of being broken into purpose, I have gained wisdom through experience, and I'm still learning by the power of the Holy Spirit. My desire to break the cycle that has plagued my family for several generations has taken me beneath the surface of events, to the roots. I've heard about generational curses, and so I have decided to evaluate how they have shown up in my own life. Once my true enemy was revealed and exposed, my basic training in Spiritual Warfare began.

My desire for lives to find freedom led me to ask for the Holy Spirit's guidance in seeking truth. I recognized that I needed to change my way of thinking. And so…

TODAY I HEAL FROM YESTERDAY TO CHANGE TOMORROW

CHAPTER 1

YOKES, FETTERS AND STATISTICS

Y oke: *A wooden bar placed across the necks of two animals to hold them together, into which a plow may be attached. Put a yoke on, couple, unite.*

Fetter: *Chains or shackles for the feet. Something that confines; restraint."*

Here are some synonyms: *Constraint, restrict, restraint, limit, and chain, enchain, bind, handcuff, shackle.*

Statistics shows that 63% of women who have experienced childhood sexual abuse before age fourteen also experience rape or attempted rape after age fourteen. *Wikipedia* explains that victims of abuse and manipulation often get trapped into a self-image of victimization. They experience a pervasive sense of helplessness, passivity, loss of control, pessimism, negative thinking, strong feelings of guilt, shame, self-blame and depression. If the parents' upbringing included physical, emotional, mental and/or sexual abuse, the child will be raised the same way, if there is no intervention. I'm describing what it's like to feel trapped in a painful cycle that seems to have no end. Invisible forces seem to linger around, setting up traps and even playing matchmaker—connecting abuser with victim. My search for answers inspired me to study nature versus nurture. Nature is that which is inherited: it's genetic. Nurture refers to all environmental influences after conception, i.e., experiences. Neither nature nor experience explained my getting victimized at such an early age, and why generation after generation of women were victimized. Psychological manuals call this the "generational cycle."

How was it that my maternal grandmother would suffer sexual and mental abuse, and then have children who suffered the same kind of trauma, even down to the second and third generation? My question was this: *was the mind of a victim a thing that could be inherited?* The phenomenon wasn't easily answered. But when I combined my studies with the Bible I discovered there were spiritual and carnal battles. I was desperate for and determined to get deliverance. "Lord show me how to break this curse!" was my prayer. We were not wrestling with flesh and blood but against principalities, rulers of darkness, and spiritual wickedness in high places (Ephesians 6:12).

God's wisdom and my determined search for answers have delivered me from the consequences of many poor decisions that I made while I was in bondage to a generational curse. Why had my grandmother, my mother, my daughter and I been victims of sexual assault? The Spirit of God led me to search for commonalities. One obvious commonality was that all of us dealt with abusive, controlling, selfish, and alcoholic men. Then we had children with them. They were the same men only with different names who were too similar for me to believe it was just a coincidence.

Having children with cursed men is like a down payment for future generations to experience bondage. I guess, to be fair, we were the same, as well. Never able to scream, but we learned how to keep moving in spite of our pain. We were silent sufferers, something we seemed to have inherited. We lacked nurturing. We never really knew what love was. We were all under a curse. I say *were* because once the enemy is exposed and God reveals your purpose the combination brings forth Curse-Breakers.

When we deal with spiritual issues with flesh solutions we treat the symptoms but do not cure the illness. We are children of the Most High God and we're in a battle that is already won! We are more than conquerors. Psalms 144:1 says, "He teaches our hands to war and our fingers to battle." My story is about how I went from cursed to freedom. God has taken my brokenness and is using it as a source of healing. The story of life under a generational curse goes deep, but I will begin where I am most familiar.

My grandmother Sylvia was born in Clarksville, Maryland in 1937. Her parents were Martha and Theodore Harris. She was the middle child of two sisters. Unfortunately, her mother died from a brain tumor when she was just three years old. Her father, unable and unwilling to take care of the three girls, allowed them to be separated. The oldest sister, Geraldine, only 5 years old, was sent to a state institution until she was 15. Ethel, the youngest, just 18 months old, was sent to foster care. But later she was given to a family member who nursed her back from a near death experience. My grandma Sylvia was sent to stay with her great Aunt Iris (her father's aunt) and Uncle Ivan. She would not reunite with her sisters until she turned 15 years old.

My grandma was treated like a servant, often getting up early to do chores and look after the needs of the other children. Her aunt and uncle had four children, three boys and one girl named Sis. Sis was spoiled and also very jealous of my grandmother because of her long hair. When pressing my grandmother's hair, Sis would burn her hair out. That would be the least of grandma's problems. Her uncle would creep into her room at night and molest her. She would wonder how no one knew, because the house was old and made creaking noises whenever people walked through it, and her bedroom was next to her aunt and uncle's bedroom.

To avoid being in the house my grandma joined every academic high school program. Grandma was a very talented writer, and a bright student—a bit of a nerd some would say. When she graduated with honors no one attended her graduation, not even her dad. She longed to feel loved but none of her experiences taught her what love was. She knew that what she was experiencing was not at all love. While in high school my grandmother met her husband, Ernest Samson. Craving love and wanting to escape the horrible home she had grown up in, she and Ernest married the July after graduation; she was 18 and Ernest, a high school dropout, was 20. Ernest had a drinking and cheating problem, a horrible combination for newlyweds. Grandma had my Aunt Renee at 19; my mother, who she named after her, was born eleven months later. In between Ernest's cheating and Grandma having to sometimes get him out of other women's beds, she would have several more children. After my mom she would have two more children by her husband, before she started to see someone else—a man named Donny. She cared for Donny, but wanted him to stop drinking. Around the same time my grandma attempted to move on with Donny there was another man interested in her.

Seeing that my grandma had moved on from Ernest, this already married man would just come by unannounced. One day he raped my grandmother, she got pregnant and had his baby. Donny, who was still in her life, also impregnated her. Later she would have another child by my grandfather Ernest that he would never claim as his own. My grandmother ended up the mother to seven children with a cheating drunk for a husband. Worn down and beat up emotionally I imagine she fought feelings of hopelessness.

One day there was a knock at the door. It was the Seventh Day Adventists. Grandmother opened the door and talked with them. The Seventh Day folks weren't just offering a God that would forgive her of her sins, but a doctrine that made more sense to her than any other. She joined them and began selling magazines to pay for her children's Christian education. When she would go to people's homes she not only sold them books and magazines, but prayed with them and offered hope. She wanted to help with people's problems; she had a heart for people. She was blessed as well; all seven of her children went to Christian school. My

Grandmother lived in the projects but she worked hard to give her children a better life. She would even scrub floors to make ends meet, and she also expected her children to work hard to help pay for their Christian education.

Grandmother's children were her inspiration for getting involved in the youth ministries. She was called the Missionary Volunteer Leader's assistant. Because of her gift of evangelism she was invited to partner with an evangelist from the church, Brother Joseph Montgomery. He was an attractive man who was married but wasn't secretive about his marital difficulties.

My grandmother was in the process of getting divorced and wanted so badly to feel loved. It wasn't long before Brother Joseph's nice and charming ways would win Grandma over. Brother Joseph, who was unhappy in his current situation, appreciated my grandmother's sincere and giving heart. And he would often come over and spend time with her children, who remember him being so kind and attentive, unlike their fathers.

The relationship crossed over into the forbidden. The evangelist couple would have children, a set of twin girls, and a year later another daughter. The church leaders told my grandmother to avoid embarrassment, and since they both were legally married to other people, that it would be best if she listed her current husband Ernest as the father, even though they were not seeing each other any longer. My Grandmother suspected, the church's General Conference sent Brother Joseph to New Jersey, to separate them. Members would claim they saw them on the beach together, to keep the drama going. It was such a scandal.

The embarrassment my grandmother endured caused her to stop going to church, but she would send her children. Grandma tried to sit my mother, then 13, down to prepare her for some of the rumors she might hear. My mother wasn't interested; she just wanted to be a kid. Joseph promised my grandmother that when he got his divorce he would marry her. The church treated him like he had been seduced, and it bothered my grandmother that he would not defend her. The worst part of it was that her children were often mistreated by the adults.

While in New Jersey Joseph would get his children and they would report on their time with their father. They began to report about a woman who was buying them things and spending time with them. The woman was nice and the girls really liked her. My grandmother learned that Brother Joseph was preparing to marry this woman.

Like she did when she was with Ernest, she decided to confront Joseph and went to New Jersey. She sternly reminded him that he was supposed to marry *her*. After all the hell and embarrassment she had been put through alone, and having borne three more children, he now had the audacity to move on...with another woman! She convinced him to break off the engagement with the other woman and in 1979 they were married. Just two years later the woman to whom Joseph was engaged would die of cancer.

Right before their marriage a new church branched off from the old church. Since a lot of the members stopped speaking to my grandma, she worked diligently evangelizing. The new church was named Faith Church and was located in one of Baltimore's rougher neighborhoods. It was started by Pastor Carl Jeffrey's and members Edna Jones, the Reynolds family, Sister Matthews and my grandmother. The church was very close; they were often referred to by the other churches as "The Misfit Church." They were looked upon as the sinner church and not thought of very highly.

This church offered refuge for sinners who couldn't live up to the silly idea that you needed to be perfect before coming to Christ. They were misfits most likely, but they really knew what it meant to need the grace of God, and they were determined to win souls for Christ. They knew they served a forgiving God and strived to make Faith Church an example of a church that was open to sinners who sought redemption. Faith Church was made up of all types of people, from all walks of life, people who just wanted and needed a second chance.

CHAPTER 2

PRISONERS OF WAR

The cycle of tragic events passes to my mother, Sylvia. She is second born to Ernest and Sylvia Samson. Her earliest memory is being sent next door to a neighbor. My grandmother, always wanting to help someone in need, would send my mother over to make deliveries to the Warner family.

Mrs. Warner was handicapped and had difficulty moving around. Her husband was very mobile, and before his wife could turn and acknowledge my mother's presence, Mr. Warner would take advantage of every second and fondle my mother all over. His disgusting hands would move in and out of her underwear.

My mother, who was about 4 years old, wondered what she had done to cause such a reaction. Around the same time she watched her sister be raped by her mother's cousin. She asked him if she would be next. This was more confirmation during her formative years that this was what she was supposed to go through.

Growing up my mother's family would say, "You would be pretty if you weren't so dark." Her self-esteem should have been better but the only affirmation of her beauty she found in the attention she got from the opposite sex. Boys always surrounded her; they flocked to her. They would talk to her about anything. And she would often experience jealousy from the other girls. My mother took after her mother; she loved to read. She would get three to four books at a time to read from the library.

When she was 13 years old, on her way to the library one day she walked past her friends' house, who were twin boys. They told her to come in, that they wanted to show her something. She laughed and refused, knowing she would get into a lot of trouble. After much persuasion she went to the door and was yanked in by one of the boys. They threw her down, she fought back hard, got away and ran through the whole house before succumbing to their strength. They raped her, both of them. She was bleeding and in so much pain. When the boys were done they let her go.

She walked outside in disbelief. She saw her friend Pat and she knew coming out of the boys' house looked bad so she smiled, as if nothing had happened. There was no one she could tell that wouldn't judge her as being a loose girl. She didn't say a word to anyone, but chose to live silently with the shame, guilt and disgust. She attempted to go back to normal, but nothing would ever be the same again. The question that she'd asked when she was 4 years old of her sister's attacker, "will I be next," had just been answered.

She was still going to church and having to ignore the looks and rumors that her mom was a loose woman that seduced poor Brother Joseph was overwhelming enough. She refused to be the victim of ridicule and suffer twice. She would just hold it all in and suffer in silence, just as her mom had done. My mom, who had this prissy demeanor, never felt like a little girl again. When she would be sent outside she hated to play with the other kids because she didn't want to get dirty. In the projects there was a place where you could look out and see everything. My mother would often just stand in this place and observe.

One day while standing in this place my mother was approached by a little boy a few years older than her. He said to her, "One day I'm going to marry you." She thought nothing of it but never forgot him. My mother had assumed a grown-up persona, and had a boyfriend named Terrance. She said when she and Terrance would hang out there was always this young man that hung out with them. When she broke up with Terrance, this guy was right there ready to seize the opportunity to be with her. His name was George Harvey.

He was a very handsome young man that was persistent and determined. When they began dating George told her that he was the young man that had proposed to her years earlier. She considered that fate, and they began a relationship. George told her about all the women that would throw themselves at him, and discuss their personal hygiene and promiscuous behavior with her. Although that meant she was not the only one, the only thing that my mother needed to hear was that she was special and somehow that made everything okay.

For high school my mother went away to a boarding school, Highland View Academy—a predominantly white school. She stayed in contact with George and would see him when she returned home. After graduation she stayed with her older sister in Takoma Park, Maryland. During the summer she worked at an agency called the National Institutes of Health. N.I.H. allowed her to work, pay for tuition to attend Columbia Union College, now known as Washington Adventist University. She came home on the weekends. George, still determined, called to tell her to come home early one day. Sylvia, eager to hear the surprise, left work and returned to Baltimore to find George accompanied by a friend.

He told her that he was going to get the marriage certificate and he wanted her to come. She didn't want to get married, but he told her the license was good for six months and she could use that time to decide. Knowing that he could talk her into anything if he persisted, she agreed. On that day not only did George talk my mom into picking up the marriage certificate, he persuaded her to become his wife.

She was only 18 years old. In my mother's defense, George was not your average kid from the streets. He was extremely intelligent. He'd taken an I.Q. test; his score was that of a genius. He had a knack for retaining information that he'd read or heard. Though he lacked direction and drive, he had the potential to be somebody. But his reckless behavior, alcoholism and short temper meant he spent more time in jail than he did in college.

My mother tried to keep their marriage a secret and continue with her plans to go to school and see her husband on the weekends. George's mom allowed him and his brother to have sleepovers with loose women anytime. So the plan was that he would take my mom there. When my mom and her husband attempted to stay at his mother's house she immediately called my grandmother's best friend, Sister Reynolds, to let her know that my mom was trying to stay over. Since it was a problem, they let his mother in on the secret—they were married. She was so happy that she offered her bedroom.

The secret was out now with Sister Reynolds knowing, so they had to come clean to my grandmother. My grandmother was not excited about their marriage but would rather they stay at her house than at Hazel's, George's mother. My mother continued to go to school and come home on weekends. When she got pregnant she had to drop out of school and return to Baltimore.

She told her husband that he would have to get them a place because she was not going to stay with either of their moms. George found a job, and with the help of Grandma Sylvia, they found an apartment, which she helped to fix up. My mom had her first daughter; she named her Sylvia, but we called her Arlene.

Just two short years later, at 21, she would become pregnant with me. It was then that she discovered that her husband was having an affair. She caught him on the phone with a woman named Karen, telling her how much he loved her. Years later my father and Karen would have a son together, Kevin. My mom and dad broke up while she was pregnant with me. My mother was in shock and heartbroken. Still, the cheating continued.

In the same year I was born my father also had a son with a completely different woman; he was named after my father.

My father was raised to believe that he should never turn down sex from a woman. His mom taught him this. He lost his father over a quarter when he was 3 years old, so he never learned how to be a man from a man. His mother's belief that to be a man he must sleep around was absurd, but she had been married several times herself. She undoubtedly experienced cheating and so viewed loyalty to one woman as being weak.

My mother moved on and did her best to hold it together for her children. My dad was then arrested. During the time of his incarceration he would send my mom a few dollars a week to help out. It wasn't much but she appreciated his efforts. When he got out, while she worked and went to class, he would watch us. She would allow him to stay in the room with us overnight when she got home too late.

One night while on her way home a tall gentleman asked for my mom's number, and since she was single she obliged. When he called my father grabbed the phone and told the man my mother was married. The guy never called again. That night my dad yelled that if she needed to be with someone it should be him, as if she belonged to him. He was aggressive, and tried to be with her, but she stopped him from completing his advances. Later that year she got so sick. When she went to see why she couldn't eat, the doctor had no answers. When the doctor said she was pregnant she was confused. She refused to accept it.

The doctor warned that if she didn't accept it, she would lose her child. She was bewildered. She knew she couldn't be pregnant because she hadn't really been with anyone. The night my father tried to lay with her, there was not complete penetration. It wasn't until she read an article about a young girl whose hymen was still intact after she'd gotten pregnant that she learned sperm travels. This was so devastating. She was pregnant by her cheating ex-husband. She gave birth to a beautiful little girl that she named Donna. George would again go to jail. She got a break from his popping up any hour of the night drunk to beg her to come back to him.

My mother kept other men around because she was afraid of my father, who would violently attack her. She had a friend named Marvin, who she confided in. Marvin, for the most part, was kind. My mom attempted to move on with Marvin. One time he came over intoxicated and started making sexual advances toward her. My mom knew he was drunk and denied his advances. That night Marvin, raped my mom. Soon after she learned she was pregnant.

Humiliated and embarrassed, she gave her last daughter her married name, Harvey. She named her Victoria after her sister. She was a divorced mother of now four girls. She didn't want the members at Faith Church to know she had left George after giving birth to Donna, but now it was out that she was in fact divorced. She was talked about and looked down on for being a single mother with another child that didn't exactly look like her ex. The shame that her mother had once felt at this church was now her burden to carry.

Vulnerable and distraught, she felt like damaged goods. She wasn't enough for her ex George and it was as if she was carrying a sign that said "take me." She couldn't help but wonder what she was doing to attract these attacks. She was carrying the guilt of that little girl that was touched by Mr. Warner. Wait, Mr. Marvin Warner, the same name as her last rapist, Marvin Warner, and they resembled! Could he have been related to her first molester? The question has never been answered.

Her self-esteem was shot and she desperately needed to feel safe. At the right time she meets William, a man approximately 6'4; a man that would intimidate the average man. He was home from the Marines and stayed with his mom around the corner. He showed interest in not only my mom but her four girls. He seemed nice and he wasted no time asking my mom to marry him. Just four short months after meeting, they were married. I'm sure she was so ready for that safety and security. I know for sure that she wanted her happily ever after. Now let's begin my journey.

CHAPTER 3

GET 'EM WHILE THEY'RE YOUNG

MY EARLIEST MEMORY was when I was about 3 years old. I remember sitting on someone's lap at church when I felt a hand in my underwear touching my private area. This would be the beginning of years of inappropriate behavior. See, my mom had a friend whom she trusted and her friend had daughters who always wanted to take us with them. My mom was trusting, very trusting of them, and even though their mother had a live-in boyfriend she would send us over their house all the time.

While at church for all-day service we would be sent downstairs for the oldest to watch us. This would prove to be a very harmful mistake because these young girls were being molested by their mom's live-in boyfriend. Because abuse often infects others, for years we were molested by my mom's friend's oldest child. Innocence stolen at such an impressionable age caused me great shame and confusion.

Now, she would not be the only one to introduce me to the spirit of perversion. There were several situations of children knowing too much. As I look back, I could see that they were traps of the enemy set up over and over again to expose my sisters and me. I knew that God was displeased and I felt responsible. My mom was so delusional, she felt like she was keeping us safe, but because of her own abuse her mind failed to flag her for danger. By not taking the time to address her own issues, instead of running from, she flocked to, shady characters. Without deliverance she would remain a victim and produce victimized children.

The next defining moment in my life came when I was 6 years old. My stepfather William called me out of bed in the wee hours of the morning. My mom sat on the bed crying, frightened of what was happening. I knew it wasn't good. My stepdad then ordered me to go downstairs and get a knife. He said, "I'm going to kill your mother, and if you don't get it, I'm going to kill you too." I was scared for my mom, and did not want to die myself. What a place to be put in, to have to supply the weapon against your own mother, or choose to die with her. I loved her. I didn't want to see her cut up into little pieces.

Flashing before my eyes were thoughts of what it would be like not to have my mom here, but then I thought of how painful it would be to die myself by means of a knife. I didn't want to die. Observing this moment from a wiser standpoint, this was a very important developmental time. If he could instill this fear in me at a very young age he would remain in control. From a spiritual standpoint this was the introduction to the spirit that kept my family in bondage for so many years. The enemy was using William to hinder the destinies of even the seeds I would bring forth. Statistics show that an oppressed abused frightened child will most likely attract someone like the male influences of her childhood years. This would prove to be very true.

My solution for keeping my mom alive and being obedient was to bring back a very dull knife. I would say it was probably a butter knife. He then said again with his thunderous voice, "if you don't come back with the sharpest butcher knife in the kitchen, I'm going to cut you into little pieces so bring a towel for the blood." He enjoyed seeing us terrified, hearing our voices tremble.

Feeling helpless and terrified because of my mom's inability to help herself or me, I felt like such a traitor, and so disloyal. What would Jesus do? He would have died *for* her, even though the option was to die *with* her? I went downstairs and got the biggest knife, and a towel. I thought of stabbing him but I knew I wasn't strong or fast enough. What could she have done to make him this angry? My mother is sweet and kind and she loves the Lord.

By now my sisters are up from all of the commotion. He then gets gasoline and douses it on the bed, all of us now together are standing in front of my mom who is sitting on the bed. He tells us, "If you do not move you're all going to get burnt." He lights the match, throws it on the bed, we all jump up, and he quickly leaves. Not one of us is burnt. Spirit of fear, spirit of guilt, and the spirit of victim now take hold. This dramatic event in my life is shaping the way I will experience life in the coming years. See, this man was so very abusive that he took pleasure in torturing and controlling us. He would beat my sisters and me, until our bodies were bloodied. William beat us often—usually for no obvious reason. He thrived off of our fear, and he found more and more creative ways to punish us. I recall the time when my sister, who was only 3 at the time, had peed in the bed; he took her face and shoved it in her own urine, rubbed it back and forth, almost smothering her. He would yank her face up, then do this over and over again. He would have us take baths so we would be wet and naked, then he would bind several belts together and beat us with them and the buckles.

My older sister developed breasts, thighs and hips fast. I remember thinking she should not be made to get naked; it seemed sick. I can never remember being beat for anything of any importance. One time it was because someone ate tomatoes out of the fridge. I couldn't help but wonder why my mom allowed this man to do this, and if she even loved us. No one is *that* bad.

In the wee hours of the morning when he was calm Mommy would plead with him to apologize and tell him that he was wrong. Then my stepdad will come into the room, wake us up with a whole new attitude. He would say, "Look what you made me do, you girls have to listen. This is what I'll do...you girls want to stay home tomorrow and watch cartoons?" We would say, "Yes we do," just happy that he wasn't angry anymore and Mommy got to look like an angel. However, I would be still wondering why, if she thought he was wrong, didn't she stop him *before* he hit us? The reality was that they couldn't send us to school in the condition we were in; he was only looking out for himself. We girls were so tired of him. He needed to be taught a lesson. I always had this nagging feeling somewhere inside that Mommy allowed him because she resented having kids and she didn't really love us.

PREMEDITATED MURDER

We can't live like this anymore. This abuse, his anger, it's time we do something. My oldest sister came up with the plan. "You know those pills Mommy has in the cabinet, they look pretty dangerous...and if we use enough of them I'm sure he'll die," she said. William always made us serve him breakfast and lunch. No matter what he wanted done he would never get up to do it himself. When we served his meals or drink we would take the really dangerous looking capsules out of the cabinet, open them up and pour or sprinkle just enough into his food.

Each day, we would prepare this concoction and add the occasional baby roach just for flavor. We could not live like this anymore. Arlene, my oldest sister, devised a plan to ensure that we would get away with it. "Donna," she said, "you're only 5, so if anyone catches us after he croaks then you take the blame. Say it was all your doing. You're too young to go to jail, they have an age limit." I don't understand why Arlene chose her; Donna has always been the first one to crack.

Days went by and nothing. He doesn't even seem to be slowing down. Is this even working? He is still evil. He is still mean, and WORST, still alive! If he catches us we're in trouble. We had to increase the dosage. Little did we know that the "dangerous" pills that we were "poisoning" him with were strengthening him and keeping his bowels regular because they were nothing more than my mom's vitamins and laxatives.

But I guess you wouldn't expect too much from 3, 5, 7 and 9-year-olds. Although the plot to commit premeditated murder turned out to be harmless, we were in fact in a depraved state of desperation. We wanted to stop the abuse, the hurt, the pain. We didn't want to live in fear anymore. We felt trapped, like we were in prison and we were fighting to stay alive.

We would go to church on Sabbath and he would pretend to be a good Adventist husband and this honorable man who accepted my mom's kids as his own, our selfless hero. These gullible church folk ate it up and my mom got to save face momentarily, until her fake bubble started to deflate. We started getting out of control at church. If you let the elders tell it, we were bad! One day my best girlfriend and I were running around the church when Elder Eugene came and said, "No Charlene, you know better." Although I was only 7, I understood what he was saying. I was bad and didn't know better. I had no home training. Everybody thought we were bad. I cried and cried. To this day I remember the hurt because I was always aware of the meaning behind the words and behavior.

CHAPTER 4

SEPARATION ANXIETY

THE DRAMA CONTINUES. Waking up early one morning, my mom decides she had enough and could no longer take the abuse. She decides to leave William. It was January 1987, the end of Christmas break. I remember William also announcing he wanted us out and told us we would have to pack our stuff and get out of his house, the house that he and my mom signed and settled on.

We packed our bags then we each went to the phone booth to call someone to find out where we were going. My younger sisters and I were allowed to put our belongings in a big garbage bag while he cut up and bleached all my mom's clothes and urinated in her purses. He always seemed to attack my mom, nothing new about that. But why did he destroy Arlene's things? I remember thinking, "She isn't your wife." That is what a man does to his wife when she makes him mad, not his stepdaughter, right? The thought of this foul thing he did to my sister was soon replaced by excitement when I considered all the possibilities. We could start a new life and go where we were loved. And finally, no one would know us as the bad kids anymore. I just knew it would be Aunt Victoria's house. She loved us, and she and Uncle Alex had this beautiful home, a swing set in the backyard and big trees for me to climb. I loved climbing trees. This was the best surprise attack/tantrum William has ever given us.

We are leaving this crazy place and we are never going to have to see him again. Although I didn't understand why Mommy didn't leave him sooner. After all, she was gorgeous and smart and he was mean and stinky. She was a princess and he was a fat, greasy troll. Whatever, Mommy can be happy again and go back to being a good mommy that loves us so much.

We made the calls to see who was taking us, however, it wasn't exactly how I imagined. My mom said that Aunt Victoria and Uncle Alex, who lived in the suburbs in Takoma Park, would take her and the younger two only. Aunt Renee and Uncle Edward, who lived also in Takoma Park, agreed to take my oldest sister. "Better her than me," I thought. Because I did not want to go there. Aunt Renee made you read books all day.

I called Grandma and Grandpa Joe and they agreed. I wasn't totally against going to Grandma's house to visit, but I would be so far away from Mommy. Mommy without William was going to be so amazing; she'll be like she used to be. She would talk to us, laugh and joke with us, and even when we occasionally got spankings, they really didn't hurt much. My mom used to be very loving, but since she married William she was this anxious, angry, easily irritated dismissive mom. Living so far away meant I would be missing out on getting the old mommy back. It wasn't fair, but at least we would all be away from that horrible man. I was so confident that we would never go back; he had done some horrendous things. But I'm sure she will never forgive him for this one this time around and I hope he hates her enough this time that he leaves us alone.

Well, I moved all the way to East Orange, New Jersey; four and a half hours from my sisters. This was very difficult at first, but I believe this was one of the better places for me to be. Life was pretty dry, boring and mundane. I woke up extremely early, ate breakfast, had prayer and worship, went to school, was picked up at 3:30, then ate dinner. The high of the day would be the *Oprah Winfrey Show*, which I watched with Grandma every day. I had an eight o'clock bedtime, except on Mondays and Thursday. I watched *Alf* and the *Cosby Show* with Grandpa Joe on those nights.

You would think that this should be an exciting time because I no longer had to endure yelling, screaming, or be woken to die or get a beating. No running to the payphone to call the police, nor were there any burning mattresses. But this took some effort to get used to, quiet and orderly versus chaotic and violent. Sometimes I imagined it not being so bad if I could just be with my sisters and Mommy again.

Grandma and Granddad didn't even watch TV in the same room. I barely saw them talk to each other except on Sabbath, so this was a whole different extreme. Grandma was determined; she kept me on top of my responsibilities. This consistent, stable environment started to pay off. I was getting A's and B's. WOW! I discover that I am pretty smart and nobody has to beat me. I'm not such a bad kid after all.

Grandma also made sure that I saw a therapist every Tuesday at 3:00. Mr. Tim, a white man with red receding hair and a beard. He was mild mannered, so we got along just fine. I didn't even know it was his job to help me, I believed he just liked playing checkers with me. I was competitive. I liked the feeling of winning. I beat him all the time. Man, he really sucked at this game, which was sad for him because he taught me. We talked about William and the anger I felt.

He asked me once what would I do to William if I could, which was all it took to start my visualizing kicking his butt. I said, "I would slam him, take his head and bang it on the floor. Then I would knock all of his teeth out." Mr. Tim's recommendation was that I find a way to get this anger out. He suggested that whenever I thought about William that I imagine him a pillow and I was to beat it up. That pillow got a serious workout. I appreciate him giving me that, although it wasn't enough because the more I visualized hitting William the more I really wanted him to suffer. When I thought of my family, I punched out that pillow.

I can imagine Aunt Victoria cooking these big delicious meals—it was always so much fun to go to her house. And my grandmother took such good care of me. My clothes were clean and decent, so nobody teased me. I could save up when I really wanted something.

I remember I really wanted these roller-skates that I saw while out at the thrift store, so my grandmother said if I saved up for them you could have them. They were five dollars. Aunt Leslie would let me do odd jobs so I could make money. I also received a small allowance f r o m

Grandma; from which I was to learn to pay tithes. I saved up and bought these skates and skated all around that neighborhood.

My grandma lived in a cull-de-sac in a beautiful neighborhood with nice neighbors and a garage. I would sometimes go outside and her neighbor would teach me how to throw a football. I was pretty good. There weren't many kids in the neighborhood. I started to get used to this quiet life, and even was making friends from church. Every weekend my grandma would make these enormous meals for Sabbath dinner. She seemed to invite the whole church. Granddad would play his music; he loved his music.

After a couple of years came an unexpected visit. It was William, my mom and my sisters. My mom says, "We worked it out, William is different now." My grandma told me that it would be my decision, whether to go or stay. Well, let's see. On the one hand I could stay in this quiet, beautiful neighborhood where I don't get beatings or yelled at. I can play safely outside with no drug dealers and no teasing from the kids at school. My Aunt Leslie takes me places like skating and sets up play dates so I can spend time with friends. Or I could go back with this man, this man who beats us until our skin opens, knocks out our teeth, fails to provide our basic needs and so inspires the teasing of the neighborhood kids, and because of him the police are always at our house. The choice was simple. "Grandma, I want to go home with Mommy and my sisters."

I had a need to be with them no matter what. I couldn't be with Grandma and imagine all of the horrific things that my family was enduring without me. Even though I was only

10 years old I had a desire to protect them, and if I couldn't protect them I would suffer with them. What mattered was that we were together.

I learned so much with Grandma. The time I spent with her instilled discipline, gave me stability, and grew my self-esteem, but I missed my family so much still. I believe my mom went back because she was sick of depending on others, who she knew didn't want her there. She made the decision to go back to this monster with all of his promises that he would change, that he'll never do "it" again, and it'll be different this time because she felt she needed him.

I could tell that Grandma hated the decision that Mommy was making, but she knew she had to let her make her own mistakes. To this day, I think about it sometimes: Where I would be if I had never left that beautiful, clean organized home with those strong Christian values, big Sabbath dinners and Grandma's determination to see me educated?

CHAPTER 5

NATURAL INSTINCTS

THEY SAY WHEN A BABY IS BORN they have these natural instincts. I saw where a baby was tossed into water and it automatically knew how to swim. That's amazing. That means God has equipped us with these natural instincts of survival. But if that baby is never thrown into the water it may never discover that it has these natural capabilities. Now this begins my journey into my discovery of my natural instincts.

I'm now back in this home that has caused so much hurt, harm and trauma. I can see things a lot clearer now; I'm a little different now so my expectations are a little higher. I have a little more confidence and I speak a bit differently. The kids would say, "Listen how she talks. She talks funny. Say it again." My fifth grade teacher's name was Miss Murray, and with a proper New Jersey accent her name sounded different.

The kids would constantly say, "Say Miss Murray again." I couldn't hear the difference but they surely did. At Grandma's house the expectations were higher. You could not pronounce words any old way you wanted. Grammar was very important. My Aunt Stacey hated to hear a word mispronounced. The attention that my speech got me, as a member of the lower middle class of an East Baltimore neighborhood, soon turned into jealousy. I was different. There was something that had changed about me.

I thought I was the same but I had experienced something that changed me. I learned that, before I came to live with her, my grandma did not know what my mom and we girls were going through. My grandmother was a prayer warrior and a great woman of faith. She had experience casting out demons. My grandmother now knew what she needed to do to save her family, us. And she would do it. On her knees she would go to God, in prayer, for our survival.

The kids started to pick on me, saying, "She thinks she's white. She thinks she's cute. She thinks she's better." They said anything they could think of to put me down. I was a target. I was hit, kicked, and slapped every day on my way home. One day as I walked home I got beat up by this group of kids—a boy and some girls. They just kept punching and pushing me. This little boy made me the maddest, because he *was* a boy. He was taking his book bag and banging it up against my back; he just seemed to be the roughest. He was yelling, "White girl! White girl! She thinks she's white. But you're nothing but a stupid little ugly black girl!"

I couldn't seem to get home fast enough. Something happened at the top of my block; that book bag hit me one too many times and unleashed something in me. I swung around and zeroed in on that boy with that book bag then I drilled him with my punches. I punched him in his face and stomach. I got him real good. It was at that moment that I decided that I was not someone's punching bag.

Now, I wish this would be the end of where I speak of being bullied, but here comes sixth grade. I was placed in the enrichment class, an above average academic class because I was smart. In my class were two 16-year-olds. My school had this program where children who failed more than two times were given a shot to skip ahead. The program put these kids in classes for a couple of semesters, then, if they completed their work, they would be moved up two grades.

Tiny, who wasn't tiny at all, was an unattractive girl who was very shapely for her age. Tiny was "fast." Daniela was an overweight, dark-skinned girl who didn't like herself—or me—very much. She was everything you can imagine when you think of a bully. She was bigger than some women. So, in my class these girls took notice of me. Tiny would say mean things to me and Daniela was violent.

What kind of luck is this? I just learned that I could fight, and as soon as I was ready to stand up for myself the bullies got bigger. Unbelievable! Daniela is on my bus route home and to school. I would get on the bus in the morning and there she was sitting in the front row right where I had to stand up. She would say, "Your fingers stink, get off the pole."

Tiny moved fast out of my class but I was left with Daniela who would hit me every day, slam my head into lockers, and punch me in the stomach. My oldest sister hooked school, occasionally. I learned to hook from her, but I was an extremist who always took things to the max. This was the solution; I wouldn't go to school anymore. My parents weren't home because they went to work. So I could stay home and watch TV. I could eat and sleep.

I would go to school just in time to take the test for the week but never studied. I would do a quick run through in the book when I took the test and I would always get 90 or above. My teacher would always say, "She has so much potential, if she would just come to school. If she could get a 90 and she hasn't even been here to learn the subjects, what great success she could have if she'd only come to school. But I figured if I could get a 90 and not come to school that means she isn't teaching anything. She had nothing to offer but a waste of my time. Why bother when I could be home safe and at peace?

I didn't care about success, I was angrier than ever. I hated school. I hated the teacher. I hated Daniela. I hated William and I hated church. I was even beginning to resent my mom, these pretenders. I felt I could see through them all. They didn't care about me, and I didn't care about them. I felt no peace. The only time I had peace was between the hours of 9 to 5, when there were no parents, no students, no siblings, no one. I liked being alone. Finally, somewhere down the line Daniela was passed on to the next grade.

The funny thing is that right before she left, Daniela wanted me to help her do her homework. She wanted to be around me. *So first you hate me, but in secret you actually want to be my friend?* When I did go to school, afterwards she would say, "You can come home with me." Even though she wanted to be my friend I did not feel the same. I only hung out with her so I wouldn't get hit again. I would help her do her homework not because I wanted her to succeed in life but because I wanted her to get out of my class and out of my life. So I was kind and I would encourage her. I told her she was beautiful. And she was nicer when I encouraged her. She would even smile.

I told her she was smart. I did her hair for her; a French roll with newspaper inside and she liked it. I showed her how to do her work and completed her homework even when I myself didn't go to school. I met her after school at her house and eventually she was moved on. Now, the funny part was that my high test scores weren't enough.

Because of all of my hooking school, I now had to repeat the sixth grade. Oh great, I wasn't learning anything as it was. I wanted to learn but I was stuck in this stupid class with these stupid people and my stupid teacher who couldn't care less whether we learned anything or not. I was bored stiff and I had to do it all over again. Life sucked.

CHAPTER 6

ENOUGH IS ENOUGH

I HAVE TO NOW REPEAT the same miserable grade. I had no one to blame but myself, but I wasn't going to do that. Anyone else would have realized their error and got to work to get back on schedule, but not me. I couldn't seem to sit still in a classroom, and paying attention was practically impossible. I began a year older in the same grade with even better fighting skills than I had the previous year. My stepdad wanted me to be unafraid of bullies.

Whenever I would tell him I was getting picked on, he would tell me to go outside and fight. "But, she is bigger" or "He's a boy," I'd moan. He didn't care. If I didn't go out and whip them, he said, I would have to deal with him. That was enough motivation to make me undefeated. Whenever I had a fight I would have a shaky hand and it felt like my heart was going to pop out of my chest. I never underestimated my opponent, no matter how small. I fought like my life depended on it. I was never too cocky and felt like I was going to lose every fight.

The day to lose never came except with my sister Arlene. I would fight when I saw people being picked on. I would fight to protect my sisters. I spent so much time at my little sisters' school to avert any threat that was made against them. All they had to say was, "I'm going to get my big sister on you," and I was there to remind everyone that it was a bad idea to mess with my sisters.

My sisters tell of a time where I was in the house sleeping and an older teenage boy was hassling my little sisters on the porch. I got right up, walked outside, drilled him with my punches and went back in the house and went to sleep without even saying a word. After a while it became so natural to kick butt, and I was good at it. Some people even started calling me "Killah" Harvey, instead of Khalilah— my real name.

I would fight if you said something wrong. I would fight if you looked at me wrong. There was always an occasion to fight. I wasn't a bully, just someone who would defend myself and my family. I also didn't like people trying to intimidate me. It wasn't because I liked my sisters so much; we didn't even get along. I especially didn't get along with Arlene. But because of my reputation people that would try to pick on my sisters, even my oldest, would back down when I got involved.

During this time I became more and more difficult. I was suspended 36 times in one school year for fighting and missing detention. I hardly ever attended school, and found it difficult even when I would want to do the right thing and stay in class. It wasn't just about defiance. I physically had a problem remaining seated and on task so I'd get up and leave.

I was so disrespectful to my mom. I really resented her for bringing us back. I hated that she allowed this man to treat her the way he did. My stepfather seemed to like that I had heart. He enjoyed hearing about my fights and watching me beat up boys; it gave us something to bond over. My mother didn't know what to do with me. She tried sending me to a counselor but I wasn't going to talk to him and he didn't seem to care. My mom resented our church leaders because she wanted them to help her with me and with my education. She believed if I could just go back to Baltimore Junior Academy, a Seventh - day Adventist school, I would be okay. But she couldn't afford it and they wouldn't help

The church leaders concluded that my mom couldn't handle her money. We seemed to be dealing with money issues all the time. My stepdad had a gambling problem. He would take our mortgage, food money and bill money and gamble it away. I believe that is the reason for his rage. My mom masked her pain by shopping. The more William gambled, the more abusive he became and the more he put my mom down. Every chance he got, he humiliated and degraded her, calling her names like whore and b**ch.

I didn't like William because he was a monster; he showed us over and over who he was. I felt like my mom was worse because she was weak; she stayed even though he hurt her children. William would steal money from my mom to gamble, then she would take bill money and go shopping to keep him from gambling all her hard earned money. Meanwhile, no bills are getting paid. One thing after the other was being shut off. We were without phone service more than we were with it. The lights were turned off several times, and William would go out and cut them back on. I would go with him so I am also skilled in this area.

My nosey neighbor, Ms. Liza, would snitch and the electric company would come out and put us back in the dark. It was so bad that they took the meter. We were right back out that night with two cut pieces of hanger and a mop handle—so we wouldn't get electrocuted—to turn the lights back on. Finally, they cut us from the poles. That was it; lights were out for two years. To make matters even worse, one summer afternoon the water man came to shut off our water when all the kids were next door.

They shut it off from the outside. That was so humiliating. William didn't even pay any bills. We should have been good since my mom worked for the State of Maryland. He worked as a correctional officer in our neighborhood; we should have been well off compared to most but we weren't. Everywhere we turned, we were that family that kept conversation and laughs going. I had to build up an "I don't care" attitude. This isn't fair and if you want to know what an "I don't care" attitude looks like it's scary because I believe, on a certain level, I really didn't care anymore. Anger ruled me because I believed my mother could have just left.

We were talked about in the church. But every Saturday we still went, and the kids would tell us what their holier- than-thou parents said, then I would watch my mom kiss up to them as she explained herself. I would say in their presence, "You don't have to explain yourself!" To hear my sisters tell it I used humiliation as a weapon. I thought,

"Why do you care about these people's opinions of you? Not one of them is offering up a solution."

Since it was so important to put on an "I got it together" front, even as we sit in the dark because our lights are out, and this man constantly puts you down, then you shouldn't mind this coming from me. My mother didn't seem to care how embarrassing it was to be so chaotic and needy.

Why couldn't you have married a nice Adventist husband like Aunt Renee and Aunt Victoria? What's wrong with you? Why couldn't you have been normal like everybody else's mother?

This is embarrassing to me, giving the neighborhood clowns' ammunition. I acted a fool in public, especially when she was putting on a façade. To me it was her needing to look okay instead of being okay that kept her in that marriage. So I resented her and the church folk that were so judgmental and not at all Christ-like, since they shared in the blame because of how they treated her and my grandma as single moms of multiple children.

Why do you still go here? We were in the Pathfinders club, the children's choir, and on the weekends we spent more time here than at home. You stay on your knees praying to a God that doesn't seem to like you much, probably because you're too weak to leave, probably because you think He would have you stay in an abusive relationship that is ruining your life and the lives of your children. This can't be what God wants.

I spent many years rebelling against everything my mom was trying to instill in us. It all went out the window because I couldn't respect her, and I didn't know how to truly believe in her God. Another crazy William night happened; he was zapping out and threatening to kill and beat us down. I was so tired. My mom was crying. He was a big bully and I wasn't afraid.

I shouted, "N***, ain't nobody scared of you! You think you a man, putting your hands on women and children, you ain't nothing but a whore!" He turned and walked away, screaming at my mom, "You better get her out of my face!" I followed behind him feeling 12 feet tall, not a bit of fear in my body. I was numb. If I was afraid of anything, it was what would happen if he wasn't stopped.

Since there was no strong father, uncle or anyone else to put him in his place—just a few run-ins with my aunt Tina and my cousin Pumpkin—I had to step up. Besides, Tina was all bark. Cousin Pumpkin, though, well she really wanted him to come out so she could whip his behind. One time William had my Mom locked in the house; he was threatening to kill her.

We called Pumpkin; she was 6'3" and from the streets. Pumpkin wasn't afraid of William and I could tell if he came out she was going to take it to him. Well, he was afraid. She had his car keys. She said, "Come get them from me." He hid behind the door and wouldn't come out, not even for his keys. She took his keys and threw them in the sewer then said, "Now, come hit me, you so big and bad!" William was 6'4", approximately 300 pounds, served in the Marines, and allegedly was from the rough part of Park Heights. He was intimidating. Up until then I thought he wasn't afraid of anyone, the way he yelled, hollered, and threatened. Then he got punked by a woman! *So let me get this straight: you're only out of control, ready to kill when a 5'4" woman and her children are your opponent?*

That changed everything. Even though on that crazy night I didn't have the confidence my cousin Pumpkin had—I was only 5'5", 100 pounds—I couldn't let him ever hit us again. He now would have to deliver on his threats. I now followed behind this weak evil nasty excuse with every bit of rage as he'd visited on us. My mom, terrified for me, was crying, saying, "Khalilah, stop! He's going to kill you! I shot back, "Kill me then, whore!"

He swung around, cocked his fist back, and jumped forward with everything he had. If I didn't die he thought he would at least knock me out cold, and I would never be the same again. I was wearing a curly weave ponytail; it fell off my head as I hit the floor. I leapt up, still angry and determined. "Is that all you got," I demanded. Not only was I not bleeding, but I wasn't even fazed. Rage now replaced every bit of fear I had of him, and I wasn't going back. None of us were. Since my mother had no sons, I guess I had to be the next best thing. I was determined that he would never hit her again. And he never did.

CHAPTER 7

I WISH I WAS INVISIBLE AGAIN

IT FELT LIKE I'D JUST TAKEN OUT GOLIATH. This man who had devastated my family was now cowering around the house because a 13-year-old girl stood up to him. If he was on the couch when I walked into the room he would roll over. I couldn't completely comprehend what had happened, but he wasn't acting the same, especially to me. As far as I was concerned, that gave me the go ahead to turn all the way up. I barely listened before, since he had no words for me, and my mother surely couldn't discipline me.

Later I would find out that he told the neighborhood drug dealers that they could have me, but not to touch my oldest sister. That's pretty deep. I don't want to skip over that. He told them they could do what they wanted with me. Up to this point the neighborhood guys feared him enough not to touch us. I am talking about grown men who hung out on the corners all day. I didn't know then that the go-ahead free for all was given for me. This was my punishment because I no longer feared him, and had stood up to him. I felt the shift, but back then I thought it was because I was starting to develop a little. Everything just changed over-night; I guess it was time to grow up. No more riding my bike with no hands, or walking around the neighborhood with no real destination. All of a sudden all eyes were on me. *"Ay baby, can I walk with you? Can I come see you later? What, you not going to speak?"* This is what I would get if I didn't say anything.

Boys and men with low self-esteem will call you every name in the book whenever they felt rejected. They seemed to believe I owed them myself because they were interested. Every corner would bring a whole different group of cat-callers. My solution: I needed a boyfriend. After all, it was apparent I was no longer a little girl. I guess you could say I needed to grow up quickly. I had no idea what that meant, but I was going to have to learn, and fast.

The catcallers were getting more aggressive and demand-ing. I would look down, I just felt so weird. Just a year ear-lier I only had to worry about fighting. This male attention was a whole new type of battle. I was no longer invisible. I was a fighter, not a lover. I just wanted to be allowed to walk to my friend's house in peace.

I had a friend that liked to fight, too. Rasheda was a tall dark-skinned girl who was a bit loose, but that was not why I hung out with her. She was fun and knew everyone and where all the good parties were. She hung out with older teenagers, and dated (slept with) older guys. I just wanted to hang out away from home; I wasn't interested in doing everything she did. Her block, was known to be a rougher block. It was where all the shadier people lived and hung out. I was socially shy and didn't have a lot in common with the prissy girls on my block that did cheers all day and combed each other's hair. Actually, they annoyed me. I could no longer get away with playing with the boys, climbing trees and playing softball. Riding my bike by myself was no longer a joy since I was constantly reminded by the neighborhood drug dealers I was not a little girl anymore, at least not in their eyes.

Hanging out with Rasheda had its perks; she would be the one that introduced me to Tyrone. Now, Tyrone was four years older than me and in high school. When I was in the sixth grade the first time, I would see Tyrone on the back of buses with the other high school kids, and he was just the cutest thing. Dark-skinned, deep dimples and he was always making everyone laugh.

After being bullied by Daniela I would go home and ride my bike and daydream about Tyrone. I had the biggest crush on this boy that never even knew I existed, until now. He could see me and even though I had no interest in the old 25-year-old drug dealers on the corner, I loved Tyrone in my daydreams and now he was saying hello to me. Tyrone hung out with Rasheda's brother, Black, who also sold drugs, but they were cool. Tyrone would drive through the neighborhood in nice cars, being that he was a car thief. Now I had even more reason to hang out at Rasheda's house.

Eventually Tyrone asked for my number, and having no experience with boys we didn't have anything to talk about; but I would still call. I would practice—sometimes even write out—what I was going to say. I didn't have a clue about how to be a girlfriend, or how to keep the atten-tion of a high-schooler. I was so out of my league, but if I was going to have to be someone's girlfriend it was going to be Tyrone's. I thought I loved him even before I knew his name. The crush was bad.

Who would have thought that I would have a shot at being *his* girlfriend? When I would daydream about this boy I knew I had no chance of being considered. I was this dorky kid that wore a boyish corduroy jacket, boys' hats and corn-rows. Sometimes when I called Tyrone and asked for him a guy would answer that sounded just like Tyrone and he'd say, "Tyrone isn't home." I'd think, "That's odd, he has brothers that have his identical voice."

I wouldn't give up, I would just keep calling and practicing beforehand what cool things I was going to ask him about. Rasheda had access to him, since all the cooler kids hung out either on her porch or in her house when her mom or stepdad weren't home. She would call me and say, "Tyrone is here." Dressed in my mother's best work outfit I would make my way down to her house. Most of the time, by the time I got there, Tyrone had just left. I would linger around until he returned. I was dressing up like a woman to gain the attention of this one boy I thought I loved, but I was still a tomboy at heart that didn't allow anyone to try me.

When I was in the fifth grade, there was a girl named Katrina, a fourth-grader that would bully me on my way home. When Katrina came to middle school and heard that I was the girl not to be messed with she would let everyone know that she could beat me, and that I was no one to be feared. I waited until we were in the schoolyard t o confront her. Then I asked her what she was saying about me. She got in my face yelling, as if this was Showtime at the Apollo. Lights, Camera, Action!

Ok Katrina, because of all the theatrics now we are both suspended. I could not afford to have people believing I was scared of this girl. I now needed to hurt her, and I wasn't going to wait for an audience. The school sent me home first, two hours before sending her. Big mistake. I waited for her on the hill for the whole two hours.

As I was waiting a group of ninth graders that went to the school a year before were on their way to hook at my school. One of the girls asked me why I was sitting there by myself. I told her why, they got excited and started to yell, "Fight, fight, fight!" I didn't like all that but I didn't care, either. I was going to teach Katrina a lesson. She finally arrived and that was all I needed; there was no need for a lot of arguing. Katrina was about to get her first lesson in why they called me "Killah" Harvey.

I swung the first blow and it was on. I beat her good, so good that there was no need for a rematch. One of the neighbors must have called the school because the school security came and got us. I don't know where the high school kids went but they were out of there. If we hadn't been broken up that fight would have lasted; so there was no escaping for us. We were taken back down to the school. I don't know how much trouble Katrina got in, but I was given a citation for trespassing and had to go to court. My mom tried to use "scared straight" tactics to get me to get it together. She told me that I would probably go to juvenile detention where all the tough girls went who were way tougher than me. Kids told me horror stories about what was probably going to happen to me.

When the court date came I was nowhere to be found. I stayed with some kids that lived with a grandmother who didn't seem to care what they did, in a house that looked as if it should be abandoned. I hid out there for a weekend. I couldn't stay there, though, because it was far worse than being home, and deep down I knew I had just made things worse for myself.

When I went home my mother told me that because I was a no-show in court I would have to go to "Juvey," that is, baby jail. Looking sad, she took me. She stopped to get me some McDonald's, and it felt like it was my last meal. It was so nasty—it smelled bad and tasted horrible. My stomach was in knots; this is where I was going to be confronted with the bigger and "badder" girls in Laurel Detention Center for Girls.

My first night didn't seem so bad. I was placed in a dorm with several other girls. I slept on one of the bunks. Every one was talking and getting acquainted. One of the older girls said she liked it there because she got meals and a place to sleep. I didn't understand. "You got locked up on purpose?" She answered, "Yeah, I'm homeless." She was at home there. The guards even treated her like it was her home. I couldn't resist asking her more questions. Suddenly she took off her underwear, so she could be more comfortable. I told her that was nasty. She got angry, so the guards removed me for my own safety. I wasn't really sure what happened. It really was disgusting to be in a room full of girls and take your underwear off.

I now roomed with this extremely tall girl that acted really tough, and because of her size no one challenged her. She told me if I had to pee after "lights out" just go on the floor then put the blanket there and they would get it in the morning. She seemed all right. So what I got was that the really tough girls don't bother you much but the weak ones were the ones to watch out for because they were looking to find a weaker subject to make a name for themselves.

I didn't bother anyone, and for the most part no one bothered me. I got a couple of eye-rolls from the homeless girl but that was it. Of course my shy demeanor must have given this one girl, who was bigger than me, the go ahead to pick with me. I was getting my clothes out of the basket and she said, "That's mine, give it here." Not one to back down I snapped, "I am not giving you anything."

I know to her I seemed to be an easy target, but she was about to get a lesson in why you shouldn't judge a book by its cover. She started. I finished. And then it was over. She would never try me again. I saw a lot of girls from horrible situations. One girl they named "Queen from N.Y." was in for kingpin charges. She was very tiny, almost dwarf-like. She was made to take the blame for a large quantity of drugs that she ran as the decoy for the bigger drug dealers. She faced serious time but her loyalty, and I would imagine fear, wouldn't let her turn the real culprits in. It was story after story of sad situations of abuse and neglect. A few days after I got there my pastor, Pastor Steward, came to visit. He had goodies—Burger King and candy.

With that he had some words of encouragement, but I was focused on the goodies he brought, Juvey food was horrible.

I looked at him and could tell he was afraid for me. I thought to myself, "Pastor doesn't know I'm not a punk." I understand now that that was a look of concern...was for my future.

CHAPTER 8

GOODBYE LITTLE GIRL

EVERYTHING AROUND ME JUST CHANGED SO rapidly. I was still angry, but it seemed as if life sped up. I felt everything closing in on me. I had always been a runner; whenever I didn't want to listen to my mom I would run, if I didn't want to do my chores, I would run.

My stepdad always cooked as soon as my mom would buy food. He would eat it, but they would expect us to clean up. When it was my turn, I just wouldn't do it. I would be punished. My mom would say, "If you don't clean this kitchen, you will sleep in it." So for about a year I was made to sleep in the kitchen, but I still didn't clean it. The closest I came to cleaning the kitchen was throwing the dishes out the back door into the alley. Now, that may seem horrible, but in my defense let me paint a picture.

All day my stepdad, who was no longer working at this time, would cook for himself and eat all day and leave a horrific mess. He wouldn't at least put water in the dishes or clean up as he went; he would just leave it. My mom never said anything about it, not even "You aren't even making sure my children are eating." He felt comfortable leaving everything for us to do.

When the whole household needed to wash clothes we kids had to either do it in the bathtub or take it five blocks around the corner to wash. I am talking about big army bags and Hefty trash bags, since we were little tiny girls. She made it so easy for him to be a deadbeat; he wasn't expected to lift a finger. I refused to be a part of this enabling. This sorry excuse for a man could kick rocks. I just refused to be moved.

There wasn't enough threatening in the world to move me. Unfortunately, that meant the ones who did follow instructions, like my oldest sister Arlene, had to take up the slack. I believe her delusional perception of Mommy being blameless, and her fear of William, made her manageable. She would get me back when no one was home. When she was told to cook, she let my little sisters eat but wouldn't let me. She would terrorize me, and since I had no control over my explosive temper she knew how to push buttons that would lead to me breaking things and acting certifiably crazy.

One day Rasheda told me that my boyfriend Tyrone had a girlfriend in high school. Then she added, "Girl, he's not going to stay with you and you're not giving up the booty." I was devastated. One day I was hooking school, as usual, and I decided to take a walk to the library.

Who do I see across the street but Tyrone and his high school girlfriend, Rachel. I was so hurt I went to the library not to read but to sit and fume. They looked so happy. I wondered what a guy like Tyrone would really want with me. How stupid I had been to believe this boy was really interested in me. I had nothing to offer him. Rachel was so pretty. She looked smart and she was in high school, too. I really thought I loved him, that heartbreak felt real.

I went back home and there was my sister Arlene ready to torment me. Arlene said something, then I said something, and she pushed me out of the house. We had a big window in our front; she stood in front of that window and laughed at and taunted me until I got so angry that I punched right through that window. I wanted to get to her so bad. My sister hated me and was so manipulative in how she'd say and do the most hurtful, sneaky things to me. Because I was so angry and easily provoked, it didn't take a lot. She would then walk away and claim she didn't know why I was "acting so crazy."

Whenever I would go off it was said of me often, "she's so crazy." The words I hated the most. I knew why I was going off. To me, crazy would have been to accept all of the madness, to *not* react to all the dysfunction. Of course, I realized my methods were defeating my purpose but I hadn't quite figured how to be heard, so I raged and erupted into fits of anger. I was standing up against the oppressive behaviors of those around me and the passive behavior of my mother, but no one would listen. All they saw were temper tantrums. Sometimes my anger would get so out of control that I would hyperventilate, and then one of my sisters would attempt to help me by punching me really hard in the back. I don't know if that helped or not but I survived it. I left Tyrone alone and was determined to never s p e a k to him again. After all, what would I be able to say about my mom if I accepted this boy's bad behavior?

Two weeks went by and Tyrone was all I could think about. He would call but I wouldn't answer, not even to tell him what I knew—that it was best for me to make a clean break. I was suffering. I couldn't help but think how unfair it was because Tyrone was having the time of his life with Rachel. She was this beautiful dark-skinned girl with long real hair.

You could tell her family really cared about her. She wore eyeglasses, which gave her this sophisticated look. Would I ever love anyone the way I loved Tyrone? I doubted it. So I resolved to hold on to the six months we shared. I had wonderful memories of him driving past in a stolen vehicle and honking, and of the times I would catch him at Rasheda's house and he would have somewhere to be. Or that one time that he tongued kissed me and I nearly threw up. Oh well, we will always have that.

One cold day in December my sister, neighbor and I were at home during school hours. We were having some guys come over. I'd met one guy when I was staying over my auntie's house; I was 12 years old at the time. We would talk occasionally but he didn't have my heart like Tyrone. His name was Duck. He was a good kid who probably didn't hook school much but I knew he really liked me and I could use some cheering up. He brought two of his friends over, Adam and Jake, to meet Arlene and my next-door neighbor, Dreya. Arlene and Adam would later date for a couple of years. She was secretive about their relationship but she admitted later that he was abusive.

We weren't doing much of anything, just talking. Arlene left to go to the store. When she came back, she said, "Look who I ran into." Right behind her stood Tyrone. He told her, "Tell your sister I'm sorry," so she brought him home with her. I would like to say I said, "Get that cheater out of here!" But my quick response to seeing him was to grab his hand and take him to my room to talk. It was so good to see him. We talked the whole time upstairs while company was downstairs.

I didn't care about Duck or anyone else; my focus was on Tyrone. Duck left without me saying goodbye. Looking back, I'm sure I hurt Duck like Tyrone hurt me but I couldn't help who I loved. We stayed inside my room until school let out. I gave him some money to get us two chicken boxes then he stayed until right before my mom came home. He told me he loved me, and that he and Rachel weren't really like that.

He tried to get my source of info but I told him I saw you both. He said, "I was helping her that day." So, what I saw with my own eyes was inaccurate. "Okay, I believe you," I lied. I needed to believe him so I didn't have to admit that I was like my mom. I got to be with the boy I loved and bash my mom at the same time, guilt-free. Life was looking up.

That day was a Friday and Tyrone and I had decided to hook school together that Monday. I thought about our relationship, and how I never wanted to lose his interest again. I thought about what Rasheda said and this time I was going to keep this boy and he was going to love me. I decided that day to lose my virginity on Monday. I taped some *Jodeci* and *Boyz II Men* songs, and rehearsed my seductive moves. I wanted everything to be perfect because this was a special day.

I was making a conscious decision to become a woman and leave the little girl behind. It was December 1990. Well, on the Monday things didn't go as smoothly as I had planned. It wasn't the least bit romantic or pleasurable. I gave something away I could never get back. I weighed all of the pros and cons. I was sure it would bring us closer. It just wasn't what I expected at all. In fact, it was bad. It didn't feel good. It didn't make me feel more in love.

As a matter of fact, whenever he left I felt tired and sad. I would stay in dark rooms all day. My mood changed as well. Now I wasn't just angry with a cause, I was mean. I didn't know how to verbalize it then but I could tell I wasn't the same anymore, and I hadn't changed for the better. I was even more disrespectful to my mom. I would call her a whore whenever I sensed she had been intimate with my stepdad, and would stop speaking to her for days.

I didn't want to go outside during the day because I felt ugly. I could see every ugly flaw I had. I'd obsess, thinking, "I'm so ugly and my skin looks horrible." Feelings of guilt, shame and emptiness would wash over me suddenly. I was seeing things in the mirror. "Maybe I really am crazy," I thought. I asked my two little sisters to join me in the mirror to see if they could see what I saw. I instructed them to keep looking in the mirror, at my face; don't blink but keep staring. As we watched together, there it was, my face changed. For the first time, in the mirror I saw my mother's face—and not because we favor. I was looking at this face that was not my own, and she was smiling back at me and I wasn't smiling.

Then another face appeared. It was more masculine and didn't exactly look like a man or woman. This face, that resembled no one I had ever met, was smiling at me. My sisters starting screaming "We see it! We see it! That is scary!" "How did you do that?" they asked. I didn't know what to make of it, no one would believe me, and because my sisters were young no one would believe them, either. What did I really give away, or better yet, what did I take in? It wasn't the love that I had hoped for.

Tyrone began to hook over my house daily. His aunt, who he stayed with, didn't know he was suspended and he wasn't going to tell her. I knew that if I wanted to see Tyrone I had to see him during school hours because once 3 p.m. hit he was going to be outside with all his friends. The time we spent together I yearned for, but when he left I couldn't function. I'd go back to bed tired, drained, and sad and in the dark. The tradeoff didn't seem fair. The intimacy left me feeling empty, unfulfilled and unloved. I, however, couldn't undo what had already been done. I just hoped it would get better.

CHAPTER 9

I ASKED FOR WISDOM NOT PAIN

THERE IS A SAYING, "Be careful what you ask for because you just might get it." My mistakes began to corner me. I now am a middle school dropout. I was so far behind in school, I didn't even know how to catch up. I had difficulty sitting still and I stayed anxious. I gave my virginity away to a boy I knew doesn't really love me but is using me for a place to "hook" from the school that had suspended him.

I was so far gone I couldn't undo the mess I'd created. I could continue to blame my mother, but it was no use. I had no one to blame but myself. I was home one day feeling so ashamed. I cried out to the Lord, "I feel so stupid, help me!" It was an ongoing joke of all those around me that I was stupid. Since I was a little girl my stepdad would say, "You're stupider than an empty bucket." Everyone would laugh. As I got older I seemed to always be the last to get jokes. They called me "a dumb blond" before I dyed my hair blond. I wanted so badly to prove them wrong but all the decisions I made just seemed to support their accusations. I felt out of control.

Remember I said my mom seemed to always be on her knees? Well, to me things only appeared to get worse. "God, if you are real please make me wise. Show me how to study and give me discipline," was my prayer. "I keep choosing wrong but I don't know how to choose better. The things I want to do and the person I want to become I am far from.

Why I am like this? Please God," I cried, "give me wisdom, I want to be smarter than all the rest." Feeling determined I opened the encyclopedias and began to read. A few seconds later I closed it and asked God to "make me want to read this stuff. It's so boring." He didn't answer, at least not as I hoped.

Early that summer, during break, Tyrone went through a transition. His aunt found out about him being suspended and sent him back to live with his mother. Tyrone didn't want to stay with his mother, so he would stay around the neighborhood trying to find places to sleep. He wasn't looking as clean-cut and fine as he did when he lived with his aunt. Most times he'd be seen wearing the same clothes for days, if not weeks.

He looked a little dirty; sometimes his aunt's daughter would let him stay overnight in her home. He would stay out all day until the wee hours of the morning and then go and sleep on her floor. I would sometimes let him stay in our basement. He wasn't getting any drugs to sell. The word on the street was that he had messed up some money of a local drug dealer, Snoop, and was going to get the beat down. I wanted to be there for him. Sometimes I would sneak out to be outside with Tyrone, even staying on the porch of his sister's house until the wee hours with him. During these desperate times, it seemed none of his friends were his friends anymore. He would share his poetry and art with me. He was actually pretty smart and talented. He could draw anything. He rapped and was good. His gift for rapping came from having a poetic mind.

He began to open up about some of his childhood experiences. His mom, who had several children, never really took care of them and even up in years she kept having them. He loved her, but he considered her the reason for a lot of his hardship. He shared that he was the victim of sexual abuse at the age of 5.

One night when I stayed with Tyrone at his sisters, we shared a very intimate moment when he shared the real him. I listened. Later that night we went inside and were intimate. The next morning I woke up and called Rahseda, ready to share how close Tyrone and I had become. Rasheda said, "Come down here and tell me." I hadn't even taken the time to take a shower. I was so excited that I rushed down there to tell her.

When I got there I started to tell her everything and how close and in love we were now when out of nowhere Stoney, her next-door neighbor, comes in and sits on the bed. She then gets up to go. He tries to kiss me. I jump up and run to the door, to leave. He pulls me to the bed. I again run to the door and yank it open but Rasheda is holding it shut from the other side. "Stop playing, Rasheda! Open the door!

This ain't funny!" Stoney pulls me to the bed again; he's breathing heavy like he's asthmatic. He holds me down and says, "Keep still, you're going to like it." This boy was disgusting. He had brown stains on his teeth, was short, fat and he in-and-ex-haled like he was snoring. I knew Stoney and Rasheda had had sex several times. Even though she was only thirteen, her view of sex was that it was only about the body, not also the mind.

She had been with several guys and prided herself on not being like other girls who needed to be in love. Rasheda had shared that a very close relative had raped her since she was 5; she acted as if it didn't bother her much. I knew that wasn't true, though. I knew she had pent up feelings about it. I even suspected who it was, although she never confirmed it. With all that had happened, I didn't understand. I never even considered what Stoney did as rape, because somehow I felt like I asked for it. I watched Soap Operas and that wasn't how a woman who was raped behaved. I should have been bleeding. I should have fought harder. I was the same girl that stood up to William. I was "unrapeable," right? Yeah, I just had sex with Stoney even though I didn't want to, and felt like a tramp because I loved Tyrone and we shared such an amazing night together.

How could I do such a thing? What a horrible person I was. I can't let him find out. Stoney said, "Don't worry, I won't tell anyone." "Good," I thought, "we will just act like this never happened." I won't think about it again. I did just that. I never even talked about it. I had just turned 14 a month ago. Well, it didn't take long before Stoney was bragging to Tyrone that he had had his girlfriend and that he was no longer the only one I slept with. Tyrone got into a fight with

Stoney; I heard he didn't win. What humiliation. He was so angry with me and here I stood apologizing. To make matters worse, Stoney's mother went to the school where my mom worked and told her that her daughter (me) was loose because I had slept with her son. I was so embarrassed. On top of that Stoney would call me a whore. Sometimes I would be walking with Rasheda and when Stoney would see me he'd just pick me up and slam me on my head for no reason. And I didn't do a thing.

That fighting girl seemed to have disappeared, at least around Stoney. I started to believe what he said; maybe I was a whore. You would think I would have never spoken to Rasheda again, but I felt like she would be the only one who would accept a whore like me. Tyrone soon forgave me.

One day I started to feel nauseous. I lost my appetite and I was always sick to my stomach. My mom had me go to the doctor. It was confirmed—I was pregnant. When she came home she asked me," So, are you pregnant?" I shook my head yes. She flashed me a heartbroken smile, then quietly went in her room. She said nothing else about it that day.

When my stepdad got home he suggested that, "we can just abort it, to save embarrassment." It was one of the only times I saw my mother stand up to him with conviction. She said, "Abortion will never be an option. She will have this baby!" To make matters worse, Stoney was telling everyone it was his baby and laughing as if it was a joke. The reality was that it was very close and there was a good possibility that I became pregnant that night before with

Tyrone, meaning I would barely escape having a child by my rapist.

I now had a life in me, wow! One day I found myself climbing up Rasheda's back window, as I always did, to scare her. I got halfway up and remembered I was pregnant. I froze. It had just occurred to me that I was carrying a life inside of me. At that moment fear returned to me—fear of losing my child. This unborn life became precious to me and at that moment I could feel myself become human again. Soon after this pregnancy my mom decided to leave my stepdad.

She didn't care about the house that was both of theirs. She just wanted to leave. My Aunt Tina worked with a low-income housing organization. She told my mother she could get her in one. We moved from this lower middle class neighborhood to just low income. We were in west Baltimore up the street from the projects, where the drug dealers don't wait on the addicts but the addicts form a line to wait on when the drug dealers show up for work, while the police did nothing. I remember when I first saw this line form.

I figured it must be some kind of bread line but I couldn't figure out where the building was that they were waiting to enter. Then I saw who they were waiting on. Either these guys are the most dressed down case workers ever, or they really are serving drugs in broad daylight. Didn't I just see four cop cars pass this block? Where are we? Now, I was happy that my mom finally decided to leave our abuser. I, however, was pretty upset about how easily she gave up our house—to move on down—to a man who didn't even pay bills. Meanwhile, his whole family got to move on up out of Park Heights. If it had been me we wouldn't have had to move. I would have never given up my house. It was her typically weak self that would give up, and put us in a worse situation. What else was new? Lord, I'm still waiting on the wisdom here. When you finally get around to answering, please give some to my mother who needs it more than me.

CHAPTER 10

STUCK

IT WAS DIFFICULT to write about the rape and betrayal. I got stuck. I guess this is where the wisdom comes in. I hadn't thought about the rape in years, but I realized that that rape had me stuck as that little 14-year-old girl, wanting to just move on, and I couldn't. Every decision I would make would now be shaped by the events of my childhood. My mistrust of friends, the way I acted around guys, all shaped by childhood experiences. I was haunted by the memory of the violation and betrayal.

The "enemy" was determined to control me and dictate my feelings about myself. Even now as I write this, a tear rolls down my face from that painful memory.

I never acknowledged that I was raped until late in life. I never even confronted that "friend." I felt worthless and ashamed. I felt responsible; after all, it wasn't like I was pure. I wasn't a virgin. Did God allow this to happen because He was mad at me?

Wait a minute, who said that? That is not my voice. Those are not my thoughts. The enemy was coercing me into believing the lie that I did this to myself and didn't deserve justice. I had the heavy burdens of anxiety and disloyalty from my 6-year-old self, who had to make the decision to assist in the murder of her mom or be murdered with her. The out of control feelings of rage that could be unleashed by pushing the right buttons.

The feelings of depression that came from giving yourself away to someone that you know doesn't love or deserve you. Now I have to face my upcoming days as a not-yet woman who is trying not to deal with the emotions of shame, fear, insecurity and the guilt of not standing up for myself. To top it off, I am bringing into this world a little girl that I am determined to protect from all of this horror. I will be a better mother than I had. I will be patient kind and loving. She will be successful. All I will need to do to be an excellent parent is to remember everything my mom did for us and do the complete opposite. Yup, a piece of cake.

April 17, 1993 marks the beginning of the deepest love I had ever known—this beautiful apple-faced eight-pound, ten-ounce bouncing baby. "This is what real love feels like," I thought. My sister Arlene's friend Joy and her boyfriend, Randy accompanied me to the hospital. They raced me in a wheelchair through the halls of Johns Hopkins Hospital. I was in labor a total of 23 hours. I pushed and pushed, and her head was right there, so the doctor said, "One big push! One more!" He grew so frustrated that he put forceps around her head, put his leg at the end of the bed, and then tried to yank her out. I'd never had a baby before but this seemed extreme. He was unsuccessful so he pushed her back up the birth canal and performed a cesarean. Ouch! My daughter's head was large like her dad's—Kacey Denise Asia Harvey had arrived. I desired to do better now.

Tyrone and I didn't last very long after Kacey was born, mainly because I now had higher expectations. I hated to hear my mom and sister say things like, "He stinks. He smells like cigarettes. He hardly buys her diapers, and when he does he gets generic." I just didn't feel the same anymore. The little girl that was down for anything was gone. I would let him come see the baby when no one was around, since I was home during the day.

Our rooms were upstairs while my mother's was all the way downstairs. We had separate bathrooms and a fire escape that led to my room. It was as if I had my own apartment. We had an intercom, if my mom needed to reach us. I had the biggest room, and even though I was supposed to be sharing it with my little sisters they pretty much stayed in our oldest sister's room. She didn't care for me coming around her much.

I had the room alone for the most part, equipped with a crib, TV and music system. Tyrone would come late at night and hide in the closet until my mom left, if she was awake. No one but me knew that during the day, approximately twice a week, Tyrone helped me with Kacey. He made the bottles, cooked for me, and washed the dishes. I was glad for the help, but since he no longer came when everyone could see him he was talked about—he was a deadbeat dad who didn't love his daughter. I didn't want to be with him anymore, he couldn't buy her clothes or help me financially, and everything my mom bought Kacey I would hear about how it didn't come from her father. I just wanted to be a good mom, not a girlfriend.

I didn't have the energy to build Tyrone up. He suffered from depression, and when I started to pull away, he would call me late at night and threaten to kill himself. Sometimes he even sounded like a demon, like he was possessed. In tears I would beg him to stop talking like that, because I didn't know if he was joking or if I really was speaking to the demon of suicide.

I'd just had a baby girl that I really wanted to focus on and didn't want to be responsible for talking the sawed off shotgun out of this man's hand. He would cock it while I was on the phone, to show me the seriousness of the situation. I started sleeping with my mother, so if he came to my window I would not be there. I was so spent. All I wanted was to be free to do better. I started really trying to listen to the message at church. I even got baptized after Kacey was born. I didn't want Tyrone to kill himself over me, and neither did I want to be with him. *"Lord protect his mind please,"* I prayed.

The drama continued. Tyrone would try to gain sympathy by telling his cousins that I was cheating with and was now pregnant by someone else. I was doing no such thing; I was spending time with my sister and her boyfriend. Randy would take a gang of us out bowling every Saturday. I was laughing again, acting my age. One night we got a call from Tyrone's cousin, an "adult," threatening to beat me and my sister up and calling me a slut. I wasn't even interested in sleeping with or dating anyone. I was out at the movies with my sister Arlene, Joy, and my Mom. The words "slut," "whore," or anything similar would always take something from me. The words pierced like a knife and left me in tears. And just as Tyrone intended, I was miserable. I hated to be lied on. I especially hated being accused of being loose.

If by playing the victim Tyrone wanted to get me back, it wouldn't work. Actually, it would backfire. I now couldn't stand him. When the taunts and suicide attempts no longer moved me he just disappeared. Soon after that I heard that Tyrone was in jail for murder. I would also learn around this time that my rapist, Stoney, and his only sibling would be jailed for life for a murder unrelated to Tyrone's imprisonment. I gave my best shot to God. I wanted change so badly.

I enrolled in school. I was now still in the seventh grade. I felt so weird; my teacher was only 21 years old. The students seemed so little. I went every day determined to put away pride and humiliation. The work wasn't hard; it actually seemed like fifth grade work. On my way to school guys would harass me. They were worse than the East Baltimore guys. When they felt rejected they threw bottles at me and called me all kinds of nasty names—like b**ch, whore, and slut. I was even threatened with bodily harm. Having bottles hurled at my head took it to another level. I decided I wasn't going to that school anymore, I would stay in the house where it was safe. My mom and I were always arguing. I knew she was so disappointed in me, and it came out in tongue lashings. I didn't know how to do better. I wanted to fix it but I couldn't make myself try hard enough.

She would come home, and with no Tyrone to do my chores, the house would be a wreck. I felt so physically tired; I had no motivation.

I felt like there was a heavy weight on my body. I wondered if I might be sick and not know it. I slept all day and sat outside on the steps at night. I didn't want to see daylight. I know now I was severely depressed. But at the time I had no explanation for my difficulty functioning. No matter how bad my mom lectured me about my laziness, I didn't move into action. Every time I was yelled at I became even more paralyzed.

A boy they called Loco, would hang around and talk to me at night. He was my friend. He was out late because he sold drugs; he clearly had the same hours as me. I was hardly interested. I thought to myself, "He has no shot but he is good for laughs." Sometimes Loco would say, "I'm about to go get a chicken box, you want one?" I would say "Sure," since I wasn't eating much.

We would walk to the store and he would make me laugh. We met every night on my front stoop. I started to look forward to seeing him. The best part about dealing with Loco was that he had a reputation for being the toughest, craziest guy in that area. I no longer had to worry about being harassed. After a long day of being yelled at for being such a worthless child, and only being able to stay up to feed and bathe my daughter, I needed to be cheered up and Loco would give me that. He also gave me my first alcoholic drink—nothing too hard. It was a fruit cooler. I could barely taste the alcohol in it. I would forget my pain and lighten up. Many nights we would walk to the park and he would chase me around like a kid. Time with Loco took me back to a time when I could climb trees and ride my bike. At night the streets were quieter, so I felt safer. One night as we ran around the park laughing, Loco offered me some pot. I never laughed so much in my life. I remember feeling so appreciative of him, and confusing that with love.

I would get my first job that summer at a telemarketing company selling credit cards. Our friend Neal, from the east side, told my sister and her girlfriends about it. We all had interviews the same day. I was hired on the spot. The lady interviewing me said she wanted to give me a shot and said she felt I had potential.

No one else in our crew got the job. They were all college students, so why didn't they get it? I was so excited. I was a natural at sales. I was feeling optimistic. I could dress up, and I even had a badge. Loco would give me bus fare each day and lunch money. Our relationship became intimate and soon after that, the symptoms of nausea returned. I went to the doctor's without my mom knowing.

Sure enough, I was pregnant. We did use protection, though not perfectly. "This can't be my luck," I thought. "So, you mean to tell me that within weeks of laying with this boy I am now pregnant, again?" I'd just been abstinent for a year and a half! I knew loose girls that had multiple partners and no baby. I lose my virginity, and months later I am pregnant! I laid down with Loco and that same week I got pregnant. "Lord, I am sorry but can you let me make a mistake and learn from it without evidence? I can't have this baby," I thought. I was determined not to have this man's baby. Loco, whose real name was Roger, was   not very bright. He had no real future. This was not supposed to be forever and I had no delusions that it was. He had two children by two women and now I made the third baby mama. I didn't just do this to myself, did I? I needed to remove the proof of another horrible mistake. I thought how mommy would be so upset and embarrassed. I thought about how the people at church would react.

My mother's insurance allowed me to have an abortion without her knowing; I just needed to get identification. I did everything I needed to take the final step. Then on the day of my appointment my sister Arlene talked me out of taking my child's life. I thought, "It's easy for you to say 'don't', you were on your way to college. You weren't looking at a dark and bleak future." It was one thing to be a teenage mother to one child, but two? And I'm only 16!

I felt like keeping this child would mean I had no chance of having any type of success. Sure, I knew that it was a life. I knew it was wrong, so I grudgingly dealt with the embarrassment, the whispers and the further disappointment in my mother's eyes. I really didn't want to cause any more pain, or give those judgmental church folk more ammunition against her. One of the church members even said she believed my mom liked that I got pregnant because she so loved her grandbaby. This would be so difficult. I wanted to hide or have a do-over. But there would be no going back, and with every choice I sank deeper into desperation.

My once breath of fresh air quickly became this horrible, abusive jerk. Loco would have me watch his son, who was also named Stoney. Stoney's mother, Peaches, didn't seem to mind and would drop him off to me. I wasn't concerned that they were still together and assumed she knew of me. No woman would allow that, right? Wrong. I soon found out, after I'd decided to keep the baby, that they were still together and she wasn't the least bit worried about me. In fact, she looked forward to the break and that they got to spend time together.

Peaches lived in public housing with her sister. Her mother moved in with her boyfriend and left the girls on their own. Loco's mother was in jail, and since he never had a real job or even knew how to get his birth certificate or Social Security number, he could not get an apartment. All Loco knew was selling drugs and fighting.

It turns out he was staying with Peaches the whole time. I felt so stupid. I found out after I went to the doctor's and discovered that I had a curable sexually transmitted infection. I was so disgusted. I expected so much more from this neighborhood drug dealer with no future. Go figure! Feeling stupid and betrayed, I realized I needed to get out of this neighborhood.

This is not what my life was supposed to look like. I thought of my teacher, when she would tell my mom how much potential I had. I thought, never in the history of the world had someone with such so-called potential screwed up as bad as this. "Grandma, I need to reconnect to your stability," I thought. If I'd have any chance at all, I knew I needed to connect to that strength. If I *could* be helped, my

Grandma would be the one to do it. My mom threatened, "You need somewhere to stay if you won't get yourself to gether!" I usually ignored it, but there was something telling me to call my grandma. I told my mom she was right. I then called Grandma and she said I could come back to live with her and Granddad.

They no longer lived in New Jersey, since my Granddad was a bible worker, and would have to take assignments in different states. They were now in Newport News, Virginia. I said goodbye to chaos and lack of motivation. "Lord help me change, I feel so stuck," I prayed.

CHAPTER 11

NO ONE OWES YOU ANYTHING

I'M NOW BACK AT GRANDMA'S H O U S E. It wasn't going to be fun but I needed structure. She didn't say much about me being pregnant. She woke me up early to do chores and make my bed. Taking a nap during the day was unheard of. My grandma didn't *go* to work but she worked hard. I was not allowed to stay in the house alone, and she was always on the go so I went with her. We were always visiting someone in need.

She had a heart for single moms, not just people in the church. She always searched for someone that needed food. She worked to get me in an alternative school right away. Because I was pregnant, I had to wait until my son was born. She kept me busy, and no matter how tired I was I wasn't going to bed until 9 p.m. Yes, I had a bedtime. She wanted me to get accustomed to being on a schedule as if I was already in school.

I was expected to dust pictures and light bulbs. I couldn't use the dishwasher, although it was right there. Nor could

I let the water beads evaporate. I had to wipe the sink clean and wipe the table and the legs down. I didn't understand. "Your house is already clean, and I'm wiping things that aren't even really dirty?" Not that I had better things to do but a nap would have been nice. "OK Grandma, I did everything. So I'm going to take a nap now." "No, you will take no nap around here. I have something else for you to do," she'd say. I'm convinced she would make things up to keep me up. I would wait until she was busy upstairs then I'd sneak a five-minute nap in. But it was pointless because she seldom ever left me alone.

My room door could not be closed until it was bedtime. I was homesick, because there I was used to sleeping all day. I knew no one except the kids at church. Still, it wasn't too different there since none of the parents wanted their kids to associate with me. I didn't blame them. Besides, I was used to the rejection. The neighborhood was quiet; there was nobody to talk to.

Whenever Granddad was in town we would watch his black and white movies, like *Heaven for Colored*. I found it offensive. He thought they were the funniest movies made. I would laugh with him, since he loved them so much. My granddad loved me and never said much about my situation. It didn't seem to change much; he was still my TV buddy. I couldn't be sure whether he loved my grandma or liked her much. I got it, she probably didn't let him take day naps, either.

Exactly one week after I turned 17 years old Tayvon was born, weighing 5 pounds, 6 ounces. Up until the moment I gave birth I didn't know if I would be able to love this child.

He was just my "big mistake." But when I held him in my arms I fell so in love. He melted my heart. "I *do* love you," I remember thinking. My mom, who was keeping Kacey while I was at Grandma's, came to see me. I went back to Baltimore with her. I was feeling homesick, still I was not sure if this was the best move. I stayed in Baltimore that whole summer trying to decide if I was going back to Virginia.

We had a new pastor whom I loved to hear preach. On one Sabbath morning, in front of the whole congregation, I was told to stand. What happened next was unexpected. The pastor said, "For all of you girls who think that it is cute to get pregnant, it's not. It is embarrassing to your families and to the church." The lecture continued, and though I didn't hear much else I continued to stand. I guess I tuned it out. I stood there in total disbelief and embarrassment; everyone was looking at me with disgust and disapproval in their eyes. My Great Aunt Ethel was so mad she waited for the pastor to come down from the pulpit. She fumed, "I could punch him for that."

The humiliation would continue. I remember calling my pediatrician's office to make three appointments for both my children and myself, since I was still technically a child. I could hear people laughing on the other line; they were roaring. The receptionist said something to whoever was near then I heard more laughter. I hung up and never called back. After the flood of tears and the humiliation wore off determination quickly set in. "I want to come home, Grandma, whatever I have to do I'll do," I told my grandmother. "I was not a joke. And I will survive this!" I said to myself. As soon as I was back in Virginia things got busy. Grandma went to Social Services to get whatever benefits I was entitled to. She enrolled me into an alternative school, the Independence Academy, where I would prepare to take the G.E.D. exam. The requirements to attend I.A. were that I would have to attend school half of the day and work for the other half.

I looked in the paper and saw postings for a major credit card company. I called and secured an interview. I went with Leslie, a friend I met at school. We would both be interviewed on the same day. I was hired on the spot. They told Leslie, "We'll call you." They never did. I would get up at 5 a.m. to feed and bath my children. Then I would dress. My bus to school came at 6:15 a.m.

It wouldn't take long to get dressed because my showers were monitored. If the water ran longer than two minutes I got yelled at. My grandma would say, "You get yourself wet. Turn the water off and wash. Then turn the water back on and rinse. The water is not even hot, you'll survive." Don't even think of taking a bath because it would be no more than a sink-full of water. I got used to it.

I was enjoying school. I had this teacher, Ms. Joanne, who loved history. She would read and talk about Henry VIII. Every class was a new history lesson. It was so interesting, but I didn't think History would be on the test. Occasionally we would go over G.E.D. prep, but mostly she would tell us stories about the Queen of England. I have to say, I enjoyed it profoundly. I didn't really know if I was learning anything but she was captivating. I made some friends in my class, some who had a few troubles of their own. One friend, Tina, was a military brat.

The rest were troubled girls that had difficult lives. Since we were pretty cool, we decided to hang out one night to go skating. I was sure my grandma wouldn't mind; after all, I have been doing the right thing for months now. The least she could do to reward me was to babysit so I can have some down time. You heard me right, I said "the least she could do," as if she owed me something.

I learned a valuable lesson that day, from words that ring so true to this day. "*You* decided to have children. NO ONE OWES YOU ANYTHING!" She continued with how she'd raised her children and if she'd wanted more, she would have had more. I said to myself, "No you wouldn't, your eggs have dried up." I couldn't believe this. "So, am I not supposed to have a life?" Her quick reply was, "You should have thought of that!" I got it.

What if I asked Grandpa? She said, "I can tell you with certainty that he won't do it." I said, "But, can I ask?" I thought to myself, "He wouldn't do it for you, but I've got a shot." "Granddad, I met some friends my own age and I am so lonely. We do our work, and all I want to do is skate. But Grandma won't watch the kids." He huffed and said, "Why won't she watch them?" I replied, "I don't know, she said I shouldn't have had them. She said if you would watch them it would be OK." That was all it took.

He huffed again but reluctantly agreed. Well, my grandma was very wise and knew my history of defiance. Granddad would learn a valuable lesson that day. Well, two.

First lesson: it is really hard work taking care of babies so young. And lesson two: I couldn't be trusted at that time to do the right thing. My intentions were just to go skating but the other girls' guardians knew better and their plans to come out were unicorn dreams. I decided that I might never get this chance to have a night off.

I had recently met a cute guy at work, Charles. We exchanged numbers and talked a little on the phone. I called him to see if he wanted to hang out. He said, "Sure." His roommate came and picked me up. He had his own apartment with friends, which was cool. I had a curfew, but when it came time to take me back his roommate had disappeared. Charles seemed so upset because he said he knew I needed to go home. His friend said he had an emergency and was staying over his girlfriend's house.

What to do now? I couldn't call Granddad to come and get me because then he would know I lied. If I stay overnight, he would know I lied either way. No matter what, I was going to get in trouble. So I decided to stay over until morning and deal then. What a setup. When I got home the next morning my granddad was looking out the window at Charles who got out of the car to walk me to the door. "Charles, if you don't get out of here. This is no time to be a gentleman. A gentleman would have gotten me home on time so it would look as if I went skating with friends." I knew I wouldn't be getting a babysitter again. I hated to see the disappointment in my granddad's face. Nobody said anything, and the silence was deafening.

Months later I would take the pretest to determine if I was ready for the G.E.D. exam. I scored high so I was scheduled to take the test. I was so sure that I couldn't possibly be ready unless that test was about Henry VIII. Ms. Joanne didn't even teach us a lot of things that were on the test. I scored high on the pretest and knew the test was going to be twenty times harder.

Everyone said that it was harder than completing four years of high school. I felt very unsure. The day of the test I prayed so hard, "Lord please, if you could give me a miracle and let me pass this test." I seemed to answer the questions quickly. At first glance it seemed very simple, so I was sure that they must be trick questions.

I repeatedly read each question before deciding on an answer. The math, that I never learned, I solved by using the elimination method. I second-guessed myself so much that I was the last person to come out. It took the entire 8 hours. Nervous and doubtful I left hoping that I hadn't failed too many sections. It felt like it took forever to get the results. My grandma came up with a solution to me going out.

Since I really wanted friendships, and she knew it wouldn't be any of the church kids, she allowed my girlfriend Tasha from school to come over. Tasha was from an abusive household. She loved coming over and going to church from our home. She said it was peaceful. On the day the results from the G.E.D. test came, Tasha was there with me. Grandma came in with a big brown envelope, big enough to have a diploma in it. Then she left, so I could share that moment with my friend. Tasha had not been released from school to take the test yet. She wanted to see badly what it looked like.

We opened the envelope slowly. Nope, there was no diploma just a lot of words and numbers. My heart dropped. Tasha kept reading. Then I bypassed the words and went to the numbers. In one corner there were numbers that said percentile average. I didn't really understand what I was looking at. I looked at one column with the average percentile in Virginia and the other that said my percentile.

Wait a minute, was *my* score higher than the state's percentage! Praise you, Jesus! You answered my prayers. Finally, I had completed something and done something good. My diploma was mailed to me later. I told my grandma. She didn't get overly excited; she just said, "Very good job" and "I knew you could do it." My granddad was very excited.

The possibilities were endless. I could now go to radiology school like Aunt Victoria. I wanted to have her life because she made good money, lived in a nice house, and had a kind husband. I really wanted that. With all that was accomplished, I had only stayed with Grandma for half a year. My children were on schedules. My 18-month-old son went to bed at 7:30. I hated the process. Grandma would say, "Let him cry, wake him up early, you will appreciate it when you are on your own." I thought she was cold and heartless to let him cry like that. Again, Grandma would prove to be wiser than me. I had hope again and determination to survive. Things were looking up.

CHAPTER 12

I CAN TAKE IT FROM HERE

I HAD IT ALL PLANNED OUT. I had my diploma and a job. I will get my own place, save up for a car and somehow get in a program for radiology. Good plan. Thanks Grandma, but I can take it from here. I became cool with an older girl, Marisa. She was 23. She invited me over to her house, where she stayed with a couple of girls. They seemed to have so much fun. After hanging out with Marisa I knew this was what I was missing in my life: freedom. So when Marisa approached me with the idea of being my roommate, it was a no-brainer. She was so much fun and people liked being around her.

I was so ready to leave my grandma's house. What I didn't know was Marisa had problems with being an adult. Her personality got her into people's homes, but her inability to pay bills always got her kicked out. I told my grandma and she, of course, didn't think it was such a good idea. "Grandma, you worry too much. You don't know Marisa like I do; she is good people," I said. Grandma told me to save my money and focus on what is next. "Don't be in such a hurry to live on your own, you will make it harder for your children," she told me. "You don't even make enough money," she continued. I answered, "That's why I have a roommate."

I had this thing figured out. I didn't understand why she didn't trust my decision-making skills. I wouldn't even have to worry about day care; her girlfriend said she would watch my kids while I went to work. "Grandma, I know what I'm doing," I said. I moved out quickly. That weekend I signed my first lease. I was months away from being 18 and so proud of my accomplishment.

I knew Grandma didn't want me to go. She even told me that if I did I would have to figure things out on my own—that meant day care, food and everything else. I was determined to show her that I was more than capable. The first month's rent was due and I was ready but Marisa was gone for some days. I was never able to rely on her girlfriend to babysit.

Maybe I wasn't clear about my work hours, that I worked Monday through Friday, 9 to 5. I tried not to call Grandma but it wasn't long before I was afraid and I called. Grandma had received a check from Social Services for me, and because I'd left she was about to send it back to them. I told her she didn't have to send back free money. My grandma said she would call my caseworker and tell him my situation and see what he says.

The case worker told her that he wouldn't report my move for a couple of months. Since I was soon to be 18, the money was about to stop, anyway. Grandma saved the day and I paid the whole rent. She also came and took my dirty clothes, since I had not factored in washing clothes, food or even utilities. As soon as I paid the rent she returned home with the most pathetic story. My grandma told me to make sure I made her pay me back, but I was so gullible. I felt sorry for her, that she was robbed and attacked. "I am so sorry, Marisa, that that happened to you. At least you weren't bruised. You're safe now. Don't worry, rent is paid for the month," I consoled. Marisa came up with story after story and she didn't pay anything. I had to pay all the bills while she would come and go freely— all because I connected contractually to a deadbeat.

She was something else: a con artist. And, I found out later, a prostitute and thief. Great, Grandma was right again. Because of my pride I hated having to ask her for help because it would always come with a lecture.

I remember being so hungry, and at the most desperate times, right on time, God would have her bring us just what we needed. She wouldn't even say much; she'd just give me what I needed. She even started picking up my children so I could work. My mom would then keep my children every summer and spring break.

I was barely getting by; I had to take care of kids and this grown woman. I would often find her wearing my clothes. "I know your big butt isn't stretching into my size 4!" Marisa took what she wanted and then would act as if there was no problem. She brought her girlfriend around. Sometimes they both would walk in with my clothes on.

Confronting them was difficult even though I knew how to defend myself and had a temper problem. Still, I couldn't bring myself to address her. I was so angry. And to make matters worse, Charles and I were a couple then and he wanted to hang out but offered no help at all. I had a boyfriend who was 27 years old and a roommate who was 23 that paid no bills. I was surrounded by users. I stayed in the situation longer than I had to, because I didn't want to ask for help. I was a passive person, until I finally had enough.

It was one too many times that I had to feed my children, but not eat, before I stood up for myself. "Charles, get out of my house!" He started yelling crazy things like, "You don't even *have* a house!" OK, get out of my *apartment*. He punched a hole in my wall, his attempt to intimidate me. Charles was 5'5" with little hands and feet. He could try me if he wanted to, but he would learn.

I laughed at his temper tantrum and reminded him he was an old man trying to date a 17-year-old. I gave him the option of fixing my wall or going to jail. Now I would need to make some decisions about Marisa. I asked the leasing office to change the locks then went to Baltimore for the weekend. I came back home to a busted bedroom window. I felt stuck. Marisa at this point only made drop-in appearances and she never came alone. She knew I had no family besides Grandma.

Before deciding to leave I met a guy in the parking lot. He introduced himself as Travis and asked me out on a date. I agreed but let him know that my children will be home so I don't know what type of plans we would be able to make. He said bring them. I smiled and thought that was very sweet. He picked me up on time. He had flowers for me and toys for the kids. I asked where we were going; he said it was a surprise. It was definitely a pleasant surprise. He took us to Chuck E. Cheese; the kids were so excited. I was pretty excited, too. I found it to be very considerate. He continued to court me and very soon introduced me to his parents, who lived in Smithfield Virginia; they were still together. I was very impressed with his patience and approach to me, which was not what I was used to. Travis was a gentleman. We fell fast in love.

I soon left that apartment with a valuable lesson about roommates: I don't want any. I was offered a place to stay with a neighbor that had moved to a townhome. I stayed but I quickly saw that wasn't going to work; her boyfriend looked at me creepy and it became difficult for anyone to ignore. She soon told me I needed to go. I dreaded the call but I was relieved at the same time. "Grandma, can I come home?" With no emotion in her voice she said OK. During this time I had applied for low-income housing, so I'd be able to handle the rent.

My grandma, minus the lectures, again opened her doors to me. I know I don't say much about my granddad because I don't think he really had a say. Granddad learned to let Grandma handle things. I stayed for a few months before the Housing Authority approved me. Travis gave me the money I needed to move in. It was a three-bedroom townhome with peeling cemented walls and very hard floors; but it was mine. The best thing about this place was that I had come from paying $320 a month to $45, because the rent was based on a sliding scale. I could have stayed there forever but I didn't want to. I didn't get to keep paying $45 because I kept a job. When I was out of work, two months wouldn't go by before I had another job. I got a new job at MCI, a company that sold long distance phone service. I had a new job, a new place and an awesome loving boyfriend with a future. Travis had just graduated ITT Tech for drafting design and got a new job. I was excited and hopeful for what was next.

One Christmas my mom came to visit. Dinner was at Grandma's. I invited Travis. To my surprise Travis asked my mother for my hand in marriage. I was so excited. "Yes, I will marry you!" I was overjoyed, until I saw the ring. It wasn't that the ring was small. I was in no way a gold-digger, but when I knew that he could do better and chose not to I was so disappointed. The ring was gold with a speck of diamond dust, with silver around the speck. "Did he want to marry me or was it an afterthought?" I asked. "You didn't even save for this. It looks like you bought everybody else's Christmas gifts and then said, 'I have sixty dollars left, I think I'll get her a ring.'"

I was fuming on the inside. Whenever I looked at the ring with that speck of diamond dust, I felt irritated. I asked him what he had gotten his family. As he listed the awesome gifts he gave everyone in his family, it only made me feel worse. He didn't get me this cheap ring because he was broke, but because I had given him the impression that I didn't really believe I deserved much more. I knew I had done that; still, if you found that I was valuable why not give me what I deserve rather than what you can get away with? It made me aware of how I was presenting myself but I didn't know how to change it. My eyes were open and I was quietly resentful. I started to see not just what I wanted to see but what was really there all along.

I was also frustrated with my job. I was very good at sales but I hated it. I didn't like asking and sucking up to people. MCI was this cutting edge, high-energy long distance supply center. I was among the top sellers, those who competed with each other. When I felt like competing I would, and I'd beat the guys. However, I really preferred doing customer service to help people instead of asking them to buy long distance service.

I worked at night. Travis would come get me at night and drop me off then stay over the weekend. We would go to sleep; then he would go to work in the morning. We stopped going out and only stayed in the house. All of the ways he courted me in the beginning were over. I was bored in this relationship. He was keeping me from going anywhere but putting no effort in. I worked around a lot of young arrogant, competitive college guys who thought they could talk anyone into anything. Every night when I waited for Travis an overly-sure-of-himself-guy would hit on me. Over and over again I would shoot them down. "I have a fiancé," I would say.

Then one night I met my match. It was this attractive well-spoken guy who just struck up a conversation while I waited. Finally someone not trying to hit on me—how refreshing. He started by asking me about some shows that were on. I told him that I didn't have cable. He was so animated and surprised. "What, no cable? Why?" I said, "An unnecessary expense and I have children." He said, "You don't have anyone to hook up cable, not even your boy-friend?" "No, he doesn't know how," I answered. "This is what I will do, because you're missing out. I will hook up your cable. I usually don't do this, but I will only charge you twenty bucks." "What a nice man," I thought, as I tried to ignore how incredibly attractive he was.

Funny thing was, he had caught my eye before but I tried not to stare. I loved Travis but I was drawn to this man like a magnet. I was loyal to my relationship but I *was* attracted to this one. He added, "It takes no time. Take my number." He seemed to be on the up-and-up. And I really wanted some cable. Besides, Travis was boring me out of my mind. He told me his name was Jake.

One night I got off late , Jake came over. He showed up with no tools saying he needed special tools that he had to get from his buddy. He still came over to see my hookup outlets. He struck up a conversation and before I knew it we were joking and laughing. I felt like I'd known him forever. I forgot all about him coming over about the cable, I was so enjoying his company.

Jake asked if I wanted to have a drink; he'd brought a bottle of kosher wine with him, Manischewitz. I drank a little but couldn't finish it; it was nasty. We really had a fun night just laughing and talking. It was harmless, I figured. I hadn't done anything wrong. There is nothing wrong with having a friend that is a guy. He would call me each night and we would talk for hours. He was becoming my best friend, which wasn't odd since I always seemed to get along with guys better than I did with females. Unlike Travis, I actually enjoyed spending time with Jake. He had this way of making everyone feel at home. He'd host Spades parties for all of the college kids. Jake, was studying business finance and had been working on a four-year degree for seven years. He enjoyed the party life, but not so much the studying.

When I needed a babysitter and asked my fiancé, he would say, "No, I'm off and I'm hanging out with my brothers." I would bring up my need for a sitter to Jake, and he would say without me asking, "Bring them here." Not only did he watch them but he would take them out to the park and cook awesome meals for them. They were well taken care of. I would just add that to the list when I vented to Jake about how selfish Travis was when he was off.

Jake would say, "If this man really wants to marry you, he would accept the responsibility of your children." Jake loved to cook and was great at it. He was Jamaican, reggae music was always playing at his house, he made the best Caribbean meals and when I came from work he always had a meal for me. My kids would tell me about their awesome day.

Sometimes he would even take them golfing. He was so amazing. It was not long before I really wanted to end the relationship with Travis. But I felt like I needed a stronger reason; after all, he never hit me. Nor had I ever caught him cheating. But I was miserable. I felt like he was taking me for granted, like he was as good as it got for me because I had children. I just knew Jake was perfect for me.

I didn't wait to officially end it with Travis before becoming more than friends with Jake. I just made a lot of excuses when Travis called as to why I couldn't see him. Spending time with Travis felt like I was making an appointment to watch paint dry. Jake was just so exciting. He taught me the secret to drinking hard liquor. He got me into my first club and he was spontaneous. During this time I had allowed my girlfriend Leslie from the G.E.D. alternative school to come stay with me. Leslie had been staying with her aunt since her mom died from AIDS.

Her aunt put her out once she learned that Leslie had been sleeping with her husband. I didn't agree with what she did but Leslie had had relations with this man since she was 13 years old, and even though her aunt blamed her I knew it was mostly the uncle's fault. I took her in and it was a good trade. Since she didn't work I would pay her and she would take care of the kids. I could spend more time with Jake. I didn't want to hurt Travis but my heart wanted what it wanted. Before I could find a way to let Travis down easy, it was done for me.

One night Travis called, Leslie answered and told him he should come over and wait for me. She said I would be home soon. But I wasn't coming home that night. Leslie told Travis that Jake and I were more than friends. Travis knew about Jake, but because he trusted me he wasn't threatened by our friendship. The next day he told me what had happened between him and Leslie. He told me Leslie seductively started kissing him, that she tried to have sex with him, and he wanted to hurt me but he couldn't follow through because he loved me too much. Leslie was acting like nothing had happened. She wasn't in the house at the time but when she stepped in I went after her. Knowing what was up, she turned and ran right back out the door. When she returned she was being escorted by the police. Travis called me several times. I had mixed emotions. I did care about him; I just didn't want to be with him anymore. I didn't want him to find out this way but he needed to know.

I knew by the desperation in his voice that if I asked him to forgive me and said I would dump Jake, he would accept it. I wanted to stop his pain but I couldn't keep that promise. Whenever I felt sad about the loss of Travis, I would look at my speck of dust diamond and say, "Nope, I'm good." Let it burn. Travis, let it burn. I didn't like how it happened but I was free from a fake backstabbing friend and a relationship that was dead. After all of the hiding and denying we were free to be together openly. I just knew Jake would be ecstatic. He was free to love me. He deserved to see his efforts pay off. Jake, guess what you win? Me!

CHAPTER 13

CAT AND MOUSE GAMES

I DIDN'T QUITE GET THE RESPONSE I WAS EXPECTING. Jake gave me every reason why a committed relationship wouldn't work. "You see," he said, "I will be graduating in a couple of years and leaving." Jake was about the chase; he wanted me more when there was competition. His mother, who worked on Wall Street, had already offered him a job. I said I'd just gotten out of a relationship and didn't want to be tied down anyway, so casual would work for me. I was lying.

My heart was crushed. But I couldn't ever let him see me sweat. I wouldn't bring it up again. I wouldn't even call. He would have to call me. I never had a shortage of fans who willingly took me out and reminded me that I was still desirable. Thanks to the public housing authority and my work ethic, I was mostly self-reliant. I just needed a car. Then I found a car for sale. It was a yellow 1980 Toyota Corolla with gray paint on the rust patches; the year was 1997. I called a girlfriend who had her driver's license, to catch a cab with me to go see it. I got there not knowing what I was looking for. It ran, so I purchased it for the asking price. I asked the owners to trust me with the tags so I could get it registered. My girlfriend drove it to my house. I didn't know how to drive and had no one I could ask to teach me. I would wake up at 2 o'clock in the morning, when the streets were empty, and teach myself how to drive. I drove fast, 60 miles an hour down residential streets. I drove fast, even though I didn't know to slow down when turning corners. I would almost lose control turning corners, as the car would screech to a stop on its two side wheels.

After about two weeks I was ready for the next steps. I took my paycheck and went to someone Jake referred me to and got insurance for $80 a month. I made him a promise that I was going to get my license immediately, because he wasn't supposed to insure me until I officially got it. I then took it to the Department of Motor Vehicles and got tags. I walked back outside and put the tags on my car. Then I went back in, stood in the next line, got a book for my Learner's Permit, and looked through it for about five minutes then took my Learner's Permit test.

That same day I stood in line to take the driving test. The test was simple. All I was expected to do was drive around the block and pull in to a parking spot. My instructor got in my car and said, "Put your seatbelt on." I reached for it and realized my seatbelt was broken, which meant I had to come back. It was Friday. I decided I'd come back on Monday.

Later that night when I was hanging out with some friends I saw a green light and turned left without yielding to oncoming traffic. I had never bothered to really learn what the Learner's Permit test was saying. I just memorized it. An oncoming car slammed right into me. I was so afraid. I waited for the police but the other driver drove off. I wished I had just stayed in the house. I almost had it. I went to my agent and he returned my deposit. I knew we had a binding contract but he would lose his job and I had verbally agreed to get my license.

I was ticketed and was now on the hook for this car. The man I hit came back with the owner of the car because he had a suspended license and knew he was going to be arrested. After he was handcuffed I just knew I was next. The officer told me he wouldn't have my car towed, that I should call someone to get me. I waited until the cops left and drove to my friend Lucie's boyfriend's house.

Overwhelmed and discouraged I didn't go back to get my license until the last minute, the day before court. The judge suspended my license for 30 days, I was not to drive during that time. "You are not to get caught driving," is what I heard her say. I was going to and fro like I always did, speeding but being watchful of police. I passed this cop on the highway and he got me. After not being caught for twenty-five days, I get caught.

So here we are before the judge again, who ordered me to pay court costs for both cases. I made payment arrangements but my license suspension would be extended until I paid the fines. I needed to get around so I continued to drive. I also continued to get caught. With so many tickets it was impossible to keep up with my payments. I never went to jail or permanently lost my driving privileges. Through many trials and errors, I just learned how to drive without a license and not get caught. Jake would pull me back in whenever I seemed to be too comfortable without him. I would spend incredible amounts of time with him, then on the weekends he would say he was busy. I was so hurt but I would keep moving, determined to not be available the next time. But I was.

I soon had many friends of my own through work. I had college friends that I would hang out with and frequent some of the same spots as Jake. Sometimes Jake would tell me he was studying the weekend and all my friends would tell me they were headed to his house for a party. I would never invade his space. I would just find other things to do. I sometimes would go out on a date in an effort to move forward and there he would be acting in love with me again. It never seemed to last, though.

During the school year we would spend a lot of time together but during summer break he wanted to be free. I soon started to enjoy my freedom, as well. It was summer and I was attractive and kid-less. I would have the most attractive guys take me out and drop me off at his house. When he'd ask who that person was I would say, "My friend. I am single, remember."

That game became a little too real for him. Jake soon gave me his house key to signal that he would not date anyone else, but I let him know I would not make that promise because he was the one leaving. One night I let myself in with my key and went upstairs to find Jake in bed with another woman. I turned and left and shut the door behind me. He ran behind me and asked why didn't I call? I handed Jake his key and got back in the car with my movie date, who was still waiting outside. I had no emotion. I wasn't sad. I saw that this was an attempt to draw me into some cat and mouse game. He set it up, so he ended up looking pathetic to me.

I had several platonic friends that were more than willing to take me out when I felt like going. I didn't answer Jake's calls. I went about my business, and stayed with friends so he didn't know where to find me. My beeper blew up with calls from my friends after Jake told them what happened. I didn't need to talk about it, nor did I care to keep playing this game.

I had since started working at a new job. Jake knew nothing about it. I began a relationship with Derrick; he thought he was in love with me. He was clingy. My kids were still away. I knew I had to dump him before they got back. Derrick was this very attractive hazel eyed, mixed race tall guy. Women would see him and melt. He was just too pretty. Not at all my type. He answered the door when Jake popped up. Jake walked away saying, "You're already gone." He was so dramatic. I laughed about that for a long time.

So now the old Jake is back, the one that will be everything your man is not. He was working up a sweat trying to prove he would be better. I knew that poor kid Derrick's time was limited. He was so very annoying, always talking about marriage. I learned why he was so clingy. He lied about his age; he was only 18. Although it wasn't a big age difference, he was too young for me. Lying was the perfect reason to dump him. Jake and I were back on again but he still didn't trust me with his heart and I couldn't trust him. Our time would prove to be hazardous to our wellbeing, but no one wanted to let go.

I remember having a dream and waking up excited about my dream because of how it made me feel. I told Jake that I dreamt that I had a baby boy, he was light skinned and Arlene, my oldest sister, was in the dream and she had a baby boy and he was light reddish skinned and approximately nine months older than my son. We were in front of some white or gray stone steps and we all emerged from a blue car.

He said, "Well, you know it's not mine." I woke up with feelings of such happiness. Jake was dark brown skinned and both my children were dark skinned like their fathers. I didn't understand that dream and thought nothing more about it. Our relationship finally started to feel safer, but one main issue we had was his mother. Jake told his mom about me and she would say people would laugh at him. She hated that I had children and wasn't in college.

She wanted him to marry a nice college girl from a nice family. She went as far as to threaten that if he didn't stop seeing me she would stop paying his tuition. He wouldn't go against his mom, so he would tell me to be quiet when she was on the phone.

I once tried to have a conversation with her, to show her I wasn't who she thought I was. I started off by saying, "Woman to woman." I don't know why I said that. In her thick Jamaican accent she quickly interrupted me to say, "You're not yet a woman and nor are you my peer." I held back because Jake was the man I loved. I only hoped that one day she would change her mind about me. Jake let me take over his townhome to move us out of public housing.

I would sublet it while he moved in with his college friends. Even though we would stay over, we never let the kids see us lay together. I knew his graduation was getting closer and I couldn't see him just up and leaving, but I stayed away from the subject. Jake was becoming so romantic, sometimes waking me up to go and get something special.

Or having the bathtub ready for me with bubbles and candles, my favorite dinner prepared, champagne, and music when I got home from work. I was being spoiled; there wasn't much he wouldn't do for me. For the first time I saw when some random dude disrespected me that Jake was ready to take it to him. I was surprised because Jake had a very professional demeanor. To me he showed that he loved me and would and could protect me. I just knew this was what love was.

Our relationship grew even more complicated when one day I realized I had missed my period. I told Jake. His response was that we would have a beautiful little girl. I knew that I didn't want to have another child without security, so I felt our only option was to abort. After all, the common belief was that the fetus wasn't yet a human being, anyway. All that I was taught about abortion went out the window.

I refused to be a mother of three and have to deal with the disappointing looks of family members and others. The problem was that I didn't even feel anything afterwards; it was scary how nonchalant I was.

The day came when I finally heard Jake say what I dreaded, "I am finished. I'm moving back to New Jersey." He didn't even appear sad. He sounded pumped and cold. He said, "You knew this day was coming. And I'm about to make so much money." He made it seem as if we really didn't have anything special. His tone was, "Have a nice life. I'm moving on to bigger and better things. I am going to have this $60,000 a year job and the women are going to be on me.

I have to leave these small people behind." I was crushed but I held it in. I let him in again and here we go. I was finally determined to be done with him and these mind games. Did he just declare checkmate when I didn't even know the game was still on? I decided that was it, I am done now. There was more to us that needed to run its course but I would not let him have my emotions again.

He packed and left and called every night. It was clear that life wasn't exactly the way he had planned. He was living with his mother again; apparently he'd forgotten how miserable she was to live with. He wasn't given that $60,000 a year job but had to start at the bottom. Nor were the women flocking to him. He still had his college car, a 1993 Geo Prism. Not hot. You're a 26-year-old man living with your mom—you're delusional!

Jake would soon start coming back to Virginia every two weeks. It was fine in the beginning, but determined to move forward I got into a relationship with this very attractive guy named, what else, Prince. He was corny, but I wasn't looking for lifetime companionship. I was looking for comfort so I wouldn't focus on Jake. I stopped the frequent visits and wasn't available when he called. I was busy hanging out with my new friend.

Prince was this muscular 6'4" man from Memphis, Tennessee who was funny and the life of the party. He told me he modeled and I had no reason to doubt him. Girls chased him, but I ignored him, at least in the beginning. So he chased me. So many women were on him, so I totally couldn't care less but he was fun to hang out with and he pushed to make me smile. I wasn't easy and he enjoyed my conversation. He would say he liked that I was wiser than the other women, college girls included.

He lived with a bunch of Navy guys and they lived like true bachelors. They had wild parties and groupies but he would escape it, and come see me to just talk. Prince was safe because I wasn't going to fall in love; we began dating. I believe it got back to Jake that I was dating again because without any warning he came back.

This time he has all his belongings with him. He packed up his Geo Prism, quit his job and was back in Virginia where he promised he'd never be again. He came back to get what was his. But he didn't ever want me until I was moving on. I didn't love Prince but just because Jake thought he was going to come back and take me from him we were going to make this thing work. Jake's mom began calling me because her son would no longer talk to her, he blamed her for losing the love of his life. It was so over the top, you would think we were on a reality TV show. He would be at my window at night then later say, "I saw what you did last night."

One day I was at work when my boss called to say I had a visitor who insisted on seeing me. It was Jake with two dozen roses screaming, "I want to give you the world!" He had a receipt that showed he had made a down payment on a ring that was $6,500. I snapped, "Don't you buy that!" I was getting angrier with every attempt he made. I was living in his townhouse, so when that didn't work he got a key from the landlord and forced his way in saying, "I'm moving in."

Prince went and got a gun from someone and threatened Jake. Jake told him to shoot him, and Prince ran out the door. Jake called the cops. I was terrified. The cops came and asked me about what took place. I told them that I didn't see a gun. Prince came back in and the cops took him to jail. I didn't want Jake killed but I didn't want Prince to go to jail, either. This didn't deter Prince. Some men would have left this situation but he was even more determined to stay around.

Jake and I began to argue. He destroyed my things and started throwing out my children's things. He busted my TV and told me to get out. The next day Jake calmed down and called me and asked if we could talk. I told him he can come clean up the mess he made but I was in no way calmed down. I didn't want Jake dead, I just wanted him beaten until he was close to death. He thought he was going to apologize and then I was going to take him back. When he came to clean up the mess he was met by King, a "Five-Percenter" that was a friend of mine, who I called my big brother. King was 6'5", 340 lbs., with an unkempt beard and hair. He looked like he was straight out of the movie *Roots*.

Prince, who had been bailed out, and King were now standing over Jake. Jake looked at me as if to say, "How could you do this to me?" I took a shot of alcohol and said, "Don't look at me, you did this to yourself." King stood by and watched Prince fight Jake. When Jake's $800 watch fell King picked it up. Jake left.

When we woke the next morning Jake had put sugar in Prince's tank and flattened all his tires. I knew I had to move. He'd changed the locks and I was never put on the lease, so I had to find somewhere to go quickly. I called my daughters' godfather, who lived in Baltimore and he came and got me with his work van. I put what I could in bags but I had to leave everything else, my couches, our beds, everything except a few bags. I was headed back to Baltimore where I never wanted to return to.

CHAPTER 14

BACK TO BALTIMORE

I WAS NOW BACK In this state that I said I never wanted to return to. I felt like I was so far removed from the person I was before I left, coming back was a reminder I hadn't gone far enough. I was back in my mom's house. She was no longer living in the hood but in a middle class black neighborhood in east Baltimore far better than the house we lived with William.

She had a three-bedroom townhome and it was only my sister Donna and her two small children, Jaden and Dylan. My mom had switched rooms with my sister. I was not given the last bedroom because it was full of things and no one was going to move them to make me comfortable. As much as I hated being back, I could tell the feeling was mutual.

My sister kept her bedroom door closed and told me to stay out. My mom seemed irritated by my presence, and withdrawn and angry. She had just had a major breakup and her heart was broken. I don't think my sister was in a good place, either; not that I ever saw her in one. So the house seemed dark and down, pretty much the same as it was when I left. My oldest sister lived around the corner. Our relationship was never good, so I had to wait until she summoned me because our getting along was determined by her mood. If we were OK today it was guaranteed she would want me out of her face tomorrow.

I was even more annoyed by Jake, but very lonely. And I missed him. I occasionally talked to Prince but really didn't have that desire to see him now that Jake wasn't trying to break us up. I applied for every customer service job I saw, so it wasn't long before I was working. I started working for a fitness center, in their corporate office. I would answer calls and change or cancel memberships.

I quickly became friends with Alisha, a beautiful girl that looked like she should be my boss. She thought the same about me. We both smoked, a habit I had picked up about a year before and quickly got addicted to. Out on the smoke deck we talked, then ate lunch; this became our everyday thing. Alisha invited me out one weekend. I was excited though I was very shy with people I didn't know. We went out, but I looked like I was going to church compared to everyone else. I felt like a weirdo.

I definitely wasn't in Virginia anymore. She started inviting me over to her home after work. We talked so much, I started leaving for work from her house. Increasingly I was at her house more than my own, so I began to give her money for her bills. We became fast friends and every weekend we hit the clubs. We bought our inexpensive gear from Forever 21. During this time, just as I figured he would, Jake started to reach out to my mom. My mom liked Jake and thought I should appreciate his interest in me. I didn't like that he could talk to my mom for hours. When I'd tell her he was controlling, she would snap, "I don't have anything to do with that." I think however she saw herself—her own worth—she projected onto us. I did have such mixed emotions. Part of me yearned for him to remind me of who I was, away from my family, another part resented him for making me have to come back to Baltimore.

One day Jake called me. He was living only an hour away from Alisha, so he came over. After I was forced to move Jake landed a job in Rockville, Maryland. I couldn't help but wonder if he had planned everything, to get me out of Virginia, back to a place where I would struggle and need him. Actually, I'm pretty sure that's what he did. And I did need him. It wasn't long before he was offering to help with this and that.

He saw I needed an apartment. His cousin, who went to the local university, had to go back home. Her lease was not yet up. Jake told his uncle that I could take over the lease and he would vouch for me. It had only one bedroom, but I was grateful to have my own space again. We began hanging to out. And I really appreciated his help although I felt entitled to it. I harbored feelings of anger that would bubble up just when I thought of falling for him again.

One thing about Jake being back in my life meant I never had to worry about my needs because he would always catch me. He seemed to enjoy me needing him, but I hated that I did. I would pull away from him for long periods of time, then he would call. I wasn't very comfortable having an apartment so closely connected to him, so when my uncle called and offered me his two-bedroom apartment in a quiet neighborhood in Timonium, Maryland, I jumped on it. My children would get to attend a wonderful school. Now I just needed a car. Alisha had a friend who was selling a car for $500, a blue 1986 Honda Civic. I couldn't get tags because my license was still suspended in Virginia, so Jake gave me one of his New Jersey tags. Alisha had since left the fitness center corporate office for a job making several dollars more. She put in a good word for me at her company and I was hired.

When I was in training and on probation, I was up for reconsideration for day care vouchers but I was unable to take off work to go. My vouchers were cancelled and I now had big problems. I'd just started a new job, was on probation and could not get to Social Services. Jake helped when he could, but my children became latchkey kids; the only other option would be to quit, stay home and end up homeless.

I started to pull away from Jake. I was only agreeing to friendship because I knew he was waiting around for my weakness to surface, or for me to admit I couldn't do better without him. I felt weighed down. One Thanksgiving my kids were over my mom's and I was supposed to catch a ride with mom to my

Aunt Renee's house who lived about an hour from Baltimore. By the time I made it to my mom's house they had already left. No worries, I really didn't feel like being around family, anyway. I just wanted to get drunk and stay in the house. I was finding more comfort in the bottle than family. I was severely depressed and returning to Baltimore reopened unhealed wounds that I had just tried to outrun. The unmotivated 16-year-old that left Baltimore had returned only to feel even more burdened by baggage. I had this man who made me feel trapped, suffocated and controlled. I was tired physically and emotionally. I didn't have much energy left to be a mom or to keep moving forward.

I went to the closest liquor store to get some drinks so I could at least fall into a deep sleep and not care that it was a holiday. Outside I noticed this man staring at me. I didn't like it. I got a bad vibe from him. When I came out of the store he was sitting at the front. He stuttered really shy-like, "Do you mind if I give you my number? I think you are really beautiful." "No," I snapped. Then I thought about that arrogant Jake, who was waiting around for my weakness to surface.

His shyness also put me at ease. I got the feeling he didn't do this much. So I agreed to take his number. I went against everything I usually do. I really had no desire to date anyone, nor did I have the strength. But I knew I needed to not be so content with being in the house. I knew if I started to date it would push Jake away, and force me to stop accepting so much help from him.

I decided to call this guy over the weekend. We agreed to go out that Saturday. His name was Anthony and though he was lighter than the men I date he was attractive and seemed nice. I told Jake that I had a date that weekend, to which he replied, "Cool, that is good. You need to get out." He said he would babysit the kids. He gave me his bank card in case I got into any trouble. I don't know why I took it; I had my own money.

I know that to some Jake was just looking out for me. But I saw it as pure cockiness. He was so sure that whomever I went out with would not measure up to him, and he was looking forward to proving it. Anthony was a University student with two jobs, so he worked often. When he showed up at my door he was even more handsome than I remembered.

He took a seat. I came out with my trash and said, "I will be right back. I have to take my trash out." It was a test. He sat there, as I walked away with the trash. I wasn't going to leave him in my house long so I only took it to the bottom of the steps. He failed the test. He didn't offer to take the trash out for me, nor did he bother to reach for the garbage when we walked by it. I decided right then it would be his first and only date.

We went down the street to a mostly Caucasian restaurant and lounge. I knew it would be neither be crowded nor loud. We ordered drinks. I knew that after a couple of shots I would loosen up at least long enough to forget about the trash test, so I could enjoy my night. He wasn't a heavy drinker so I offered to buy him a stronger shot and told him

I wanted to dance. I had only my wallet with me so I asked him to put it in his pocket while we danced. Getting him to dance took some serious pushing but he finally agreed. I quickly discovered why he said no; he was a horrible dancer. I started thinking about how nicely Jake and I danced together, and how much fun it used to be to hang out with my old best friend.

Then I remembered that my old best friend was also a controlling, arrogant prick. I decided I'd look past Anthony's two left feet. I was determined to have a good time and so we did. I had no intention of hanging out with this man again so it didn't really matter if I got loose. He dropped me off at my door, I hugged him goodbye and he left. The next day I realized I had given this stranger my wallet. I had $200 cash in my wallet, "Oh my, why did I do that?

He's not going to return my wallet. How could I be so irresponsible?" I called him and he answered. I prayed he wasn't a jerk. I reminded him that he had my wallet; he said as soon as he got off he would bring it to me. He did it. I was relieved to find all of my money still there.

Jake had so many questions about my night. I made it sound like the most amazing night ever. I mean, it was all right but I gave Jake the 3D, over the top version. Anthony changed my opinion of him when he returned my wallet. I agreed to go out again. I didn't think about Anthony too much longer because the following Monday I learned that my 14-year-old cousin Edward Baker had died. My sister called my job and told my boss not to tell me anything; she was on her way to get me. When she gave me the news I fell into her arms in tears. "What happened," I asked. "I don't know," she said. All our family was at the hospital when my sister and I showed up. We viewed his body; it was as if he was just sleeping. I thought maybe she had it wrong. Up until that day my family hadn't experienced close death. We had experienced many births but not death. I felt terrible because Thanksgiving would have been the last time I would have been able to see Edward. I saw him at my mom's wedding in September. I took it hard. At work I cried nonstop, until my boss would send me home. I didn't want to go home because I couldn't stop thinking about him.

Jake, who wasn't used to seeing me so emotional, didn't know how to handle it. He asked, "Why are you crying? He used to tease you." Jake first met Edward when he was eight, when Jake escorted me to my aunt's wedding. Edward ran up to us and asked, "Who is this? Is he your third baby's father?" Then he ran off. I chased him as he yelled, "You have two kids and *three* baby daddies!" After that conversation with Jake, I was done! He was such an insensitive jerk.

Anthony called and wanted to know why he hadn't heard from me and I told him. He asked if he could come see me and bring me anything. "Yes," I answered. He brought me flowers and a sympathy card. I would not go out with Anthony for several more weeks, but eventually I was ready to see him again. We talked on the phone and he would come get me to take me out. I didn't want to see him but twice a week. He, however, wanted to come over every day and we would argue about it. He drained me. He was needy and insecure. I introduced him to my girlfriend Alisha and she could not stand him. He asked me a hundred and one questions whenever I was with my friend. He'd call me and keep me on the phone for hours. I don't know why I stayed in this relationship. His presence robbed me of my peace. He wasn't happy. He didn't know how to just relax.

He was very sweet the first few months. Our first Valentine's Day he sent a humongous mink teddy bear, roses and chocolates to my job. I thought he was sweet for going above and beyond but I would soon learn he was marking his territory. I didn't want to see him during the week because I had to get up early. I needed him to be up before my kids. Plus he snored.

So I didn't sleep at all when he visited. I think he assumed that I cheated every free second I had. I felt bad for him because I thought that his insecurities came from being heartbroken by another woman, so instead of tossing him aside I was determined to show him what having a loyal woman felt like. I learned that his insecurities were because of him and him alone. There wasn't enough love in the world that could give him what he lacked. This relationship would teach me so much more than I ever wanted to learn.

CHAPTER 15

SURVIVOR OR VICTIM

I HAD A GREATER TOLERANCE for disrespect because of what I saw my mom go through with William. Anthony, I thought wasn't abusive because he hadn't tried to kill me. I had no other barometer by which to measure a man. I wish I had been able to pick up on all of the subtle signs of abuse. I wish I could have known what I was dealing with. Looking back, Anthony let me know who sent him but I ignored that "still small" voice.

Anthony was a college student that got good grades. He wasn't a deadbeat; in fact, he had two jobs. To top it off, his parents were still together. I didn't have that. He had two children, girls; but he told me, his daughters' mom moved away because he didn't want to be with her anymore. He called her crazy, and talked about how he truly missed his kids. I understood why he was insecure and needy, she must have done a work on him.

"Poor guy," I thought, "I can love him better." It became very evident that this was not going to be an easy project but I was no weakling. I would restore his faith in relationships. The plus was that his presence caused Jake to back off. It showed his arrogant butt that he could not own me. Anthony would take me out every weekend he didn't have to work. He would take me out and order me plenty of drinks. It was a good thing because I doubt that I would have had fun with him otherwise. I couldn't stop comparing him to Jake.

In comparison, Anthony was no fun at all but I was determined to look past that small detail. Drinking got me through time with him. I would have him over when my sister babysat the kids. Anthony was so into sports. So while he watched the games, I would escape to my favorite place—the tub. There I found peace. When the games were over he needed attention and would ask me to come out.

At this point I was getting into a routine, not out of desire but because I thought the relationship had potential. I thought it had potential not because I enjoyed it and I was getting my needs met, but I'd decided that at least it was better than what I had been through. And I should, after all, settle down for my children's sake. I know, it sounds like a business arrangement, but I was drained. This single mother thing was too hard and I wasn't going to continue to rely on Jake.

No matter what he did I knew he believed it was more important to control me than love me. I just wanted to be in a normal relationship. I didn't trust my decisions, so I chose with my mind and not my heart. That would prove to be the worst way to choose a relationship. Turns out I couldn't trust my mind, either. I had no point of reference. Anthony wanted me to be in the house when I was out, or I needed to call him. The checking in all day, ugh! I refused to reciprocate. I enjoyed being away from him; it was a nice break. When I'd go out with Alisha he would start an argument. "Why didn't you call me!" or "Why didn't you answer the phone!" he'd shout. I can't say he was completely off because I did drink a lot, and when Alisha and I went out, I drank so much that by the end of the night I was trying to find my way around the house without falling.

Our friendship was awesome. I loved to dance and drink and she loved the same, and so best friends we were. Anthony wouldn't mind me being drunk with him but away from him he hated it. He started to complain that I drank too much. "Oh no, he's trying to control me," I thought. "If you want us to draw closer, telling me about my drinking is not going to help your case, buddy," I said to myself.

My girl Alisha was right there to agree that he was controlling, that he didn't want me to have any fun. "I am only 23, let me live," I pleaded. I think he realized that I could do with him or without him. He wanted to stay over every night; I wanted to schedule him two times a week. I wasn't going anywhere. I just liked being alone. I was not like most females he had encountered, which, I believe, made him even more suspicious of me. I didn't need or want another boyfriend; he was more than enough. It was hard for him to believe that I simply liked having time to myself.

Anthony took me out one night, downtown. There was a man taking photos. We decide to take a photo and he tells me to pose bending over in front of him. I was appalled. I said, "I am your girlfriend, not your whore. I don't pose like that!" We took the photo as I demanded, with me standing up. He wanted to argue about it. I couldn't believe he would even think to put me in a position like that. I demanded that he take me home. For days I didn't speak to him. Since I didn't call, he soon broke down and begged for my forgiveness. I accepted, again, as I made excuses for his behavior. I blamed it on his last woman, that she'd hurt him so he was only acting out. This bad behavior wasn't really him, I said.

One day Anthony picked me up from my sister's; he was wearing a dress shirt, a tie and carrying roses. My sister opened the door then shut it in his face. She said he is not for you; he is evil. I was so embarrassed. She didn't even know him. I hated when she played psychic. I opened the door, and left with Anthony. He took me to a nice Italian restaurant where I quickly ordered my three shots of top shelf liquor. I always needed to be faded to enjoy my time with him.

About this time I enjoyed getting wasted to avoid thinking about all the things I had to worry about. I got stoned with Alisha when we went out, although I didn't need to, to enjoy her company. But this dude I was attempting to love had no sense of humor. I'd make jokes he never seemed to get. Being a single mom was getting more difficult by the day. I had this new job where I made more money, but still not enough. I no longer received day care vouchers. My 9- and 7-year-old children were latchkey kids. They'd be home alone for two hours before I got home. It was legal for me to have Kacey home alone but she wasn't supposed to babysit. I had no choice so I thought it would be fine. It was what I had to do to survive. My increase in income wasn't enough but it allowed us to stay living in the County of Baltimore, which meant a better school system.

One night Anthony came over, he wanted me to be intimate with him. I said I was tired and didn't feel like it. He argued with me as if it was my duty. He was bent on teaching me a lesson, so he got up and walked out. I told him don't come back. That was so telling about his character. This I refused to tolerate. I had no desire to speak to him again. I sure didn't need him. I was doing what I had, to survive. I hadn't asked him for bill money or anything else, not one time.

I chose not to start any bad habits that would lead him to think I needed him, like Jake had. During the three weeks that I didn't speak to him my car was towed because Jake took his tags back. I had to figure out a way to get all the way to Owings Mills from Timonium, Maryland, without a car. I had to walk a mile, catch two hours of buses and subways, and then walk half a mile to work. I did what I had to do to keep my job.

Consequently, my son had to put himself on his afternoon bus. With great fear I would dress him and prep him for that experience. Kacey was very responsible for her age, so they would be fine getting home. My daughter even knew how to use the microwave. Every day I was worried out of my mind but I had no one that I could ask for help. I could imagine Jake, so sure that if he made things difficult I would run back to him for his help. Whether I was with or without Anthony, Jake could kick rocks.

It was difficult for me to get home because the buses in Owings Mills stopped running after a certain time. Many times I was stranded at work unless someone came and got me. I sometimes would have to wait at Alisha's apartment, which was close to work, until I found a ride. If I lost my job I would lose my apartment. I didn't know what to do, but I knew something had to give.

It did. Someone reported me for having the children in the house alone. The cop called me from my home and asked if I could get a family member to come get them. He was very understanding, he said his mother was a single mom, and he and his brothers were latchkey kids. He wasn't going to take it further. I just needed to call my family. Then he took my children with him to McDonald's as he waited. I first called my mom, and she stated she wasn't able to come.

I was so angry that I couldn't rely on her but if it was my sister calling she would jump. That was exactly why I didn't like asking her. I tried my sisters, even though I doubted that anyone would help me. I called my daughters' godfather. He said he wouldn't be available until 12 a.m. It was 6 p.m. I had no way to get home; once again I was stranded at work. Desperate, I called Anthony. I said, "I have a big favor to ask, are you available?" He asked. What was it?" When I told him he said he couldn't help me.

So the cop ended up taking the kids back to the station, something he was trying to avoid. I felt so helpless, and horrible. I didn't even know how I was going to avoid another event without falling further under. I hated that I couldn't rely on my mother no matter how serious the situation. The cop had no choice but to give me a citation. I had taken over my uncle's apartment and we had a new mailman. Because my name wasn't on the mailbox he returned my mail. My court date came, but because my mail had been returned I missed it.

A warrant was issued for my arrest. I didn't know I had a warrant until two bounty hunters barged into my house and arrested me. The cop didn't want to turn me in but was made to by his supervisor. The cop started coming to my house and taking my kids to the Pal Center, a center for latchkey kids. He was a really nice officer. I couldn't understand how he could be so nice while my family was so disinterested.

I was now in jail and needed to be bailed out. I didn't think to call my mother. I called Anthony. He came and bailed me out. I promised him I would pay him back; and I did as quickly as I could. I hated anyone doing anything for me. I so badly wanted to be self-sufficient. I wanted to do this on my own. Still, I knew I needed someone. Anthony didn't look so bad after all. He did come through for me. I felt beat down.

My bubble had just been busted. It had to get better. I couldn't take anymore. I was drowning and had no idea how to keep my head afloat. All I knew to do was to hold on to my job. I gave Anthony another chance. And he started really getting comfortable being a jerk. Just when I thought it couldn't get any worse, I started having that nauseous feeling. I went to the doctors and sure enough I was pregnant. I felt so discouraged. I didn't want to have this baby, and I wasn't. I couldn't imagine what I would do with another baby.

Anthony was being a mean jerk to me and I knew he was cheating on me. I knew we were on our last leg in this relationship, but I needed the rides to work that he provided. I also was going to need help getting an abortion. One night while in the bathtub I saw blood. I called Anthony to take me to the ER. He said, "I'm on my way." He never showed up. The next day he came and laid down like he didn't want to talk. I let him. Then I took his phone and read his text messages.

I had all the proof I needed. His messages revealed that he was with another woman. I woke him up and showed him my proof. "So you couldn't come get me to take me to the hospital as I was having a miscarriage because you were with another woman." He looked shocked but couldn't lie. He said, "I am so sorry. I started seeing her when we were broken up. I don't want to lose you. What do I need to do?" I told him to call her in front of me and tell her you have a girlfriend. He told her he really loved me and he didn't mean to lead her on but he wanted to stay in his relationship.

She said she understood. I was satisfied enough that it was over. I had him take me to the ER. I wasn't in a hurry since I wasn't trying to save my pregnancy. The hospital staff saw no evidence that I was still pregnant, but I could be very early so they measured me by my hormone levels. If they had fallen, then I had in fact miscarried. The doctors told me to come back to confirm that I had passed everything, I didn't see the need, since they just confirmed my miscarriage and I felt that was good enough.

My oldest sister Arlene had just had a baby, a beautiful Indian complexioned boy named Joshua. Jake would occasionally call to see if I needed him yet. I made sure every time he called I told him how good everything was even if it wasn't. I told him this particular time that my sister had a baby boy. He said, "Wow, that means you are about to have yours." I didn't know what he was talking about. "I am not having any babies," I said.

He reminded me of that dream I'd had, when I was in a blue car and my baby boy was nine months younger than my sister's. I remembered he was light-skinned, the complexion of Arlene's baby. Did I just have a prophetic dream? I couldn't stop thinking about it. I remembered how happy I was. Could it mean that I should try a little harder in my relationship with Anthony? I guess it wasn't completely accurate but it had to have meant something. A few weeks later I was feeling nauseous again. I made an appointment and discovered that I was still pregnant.

How in the world did that happen? To this day I am not sure. I couldn't believe this. I was back having to make some hard decisions that just got more complicated now that I knew I'd seen this baby in my dream. I can't afford to have a baby, not with this jerk. I don't want to be with him forever. This was going to be over soon enough. To top it off, I was so sick. I couldn't keep chips down. I threw up everything. What is the solution, I wondered, I didn't want to have another child until I was stable and married. And I didn't want to marry that man. I made the appointment for the abortion, but I would not show up because the night before I would again see my unborn son in my dreams. I knew this baby boy and I loved him. I couldn't just think of him as an undeveloped fetus. I *saw* him already. Anthony says we are going to get married, anyway, and I think, "I have no intentions of marrying you." He said let's just get married.

I thought of the dream and thought of my past relationships and it seemed like the best thing. I agreed to marry him as long as it was before the baby got here. I wasn't ready and he wasn't ready but in 2002 I became Mrs. Davis. I was crying earlier but decided I was going to make the best of this and welcome our son. So far our relationship was more of a chore than a desire but I hoped that this would change things.

CHAPTER 16

WHO DID I MARRY?

ANTHONY AND I WERE MARRIED in my mom and new stepdad's home surrounded by our immediate family. We went on a cruise to Cozumel, Mexico for our honeymoon. On the day before it was time to leave for home my new husband drank a whole bottle of vodka and threatened to jump overboard. That let me know that he was just as excited as I was about our nuptials. I truly wanted to be a good wife and make this work. After all, he wasn't just a boyfriend, he's my husband. We returned to my apartment to live our life and prepare for our upcoming baby boy.

I was due in April. He owed $5,000 on his 1997 Nissan Maxima, so I decided that since we were a team I would give him my income tax refund to pay off his debt so that we could save for a house. I had no idea that drama was lurking just around the corner. I was home with my new hubby when we got in an argument about his porn movies being left out where the kids could see them.

When Anthony got upset he would go to his mother and father's apartment to avoid dealing with the matter. I didn't understand why his parents didn't insist that he go home and work it out with his wife. They were big enablers, so he got to run off whenever he didn't get his way. I refused to be controlled by his threats to leave so I told him I would help him pack.

I was eight months pregnant by then. I started to take his clothes out of the closet. He says sternly, "Don't touch my clothes again." I said, "Or what?" as I grabbed his hats and put them in his suitcase. He balled up his fist and punched me in my eye. I collapsed onto the floor and laid there in total shock. "Surely this argument was not that serious," I thought. My thoughts were racing. Why did he just hit me like that? I thought about getting up and defending myself but held back because of my unborn son.

I didn't know what to expect so I stayed still. As I lay there in disbelief, my husband walked out the room. When he came back, I was preparing for his "I'm so sorry" and "I don't know what just came over me" speech. What he said next surprised me more than the punch to the face. He said, "Don't call the police or you won't have any money for your baby." Then he walked out of the house. Wait, What? No remorse, WOW. Who did I just marry?

I was afraid because that was heartless and cold. He didn't even appear angry when he hit me, but calculated and emotionless. I knew that if there were no consequences, he would do it again. The police arrived and he returned. I guess he hadn't gone far. He came in, talked to them and they said, "OK, it got a little heated. You need to stay somewhere else tonight." I have a black eye and a fat belly and they thought all he needed was to get some air!

It was February and we were recovering from a snow storm. I go outside to my car, so I can go to my sister's house and my car was gone. Anthony was still in the neighborhood because he was hiding my car. This jerk was trying to make me lose my job. I had such a hard time with my pregnancy.

I was always sick and had a very risky pregnancy. I missed so much time from work that I was placed on probation for a year, which meant if I missed one day, or was even late, I would be fired. My husband knew that, so he was deliberately trying to cause me to lose my job. I called my younger sister Donna; she came out in the horrible weather and drove me to the police station to report the officers and get a warrant for my new husband's arrest.

Because of my pregnancy and the stress I was able to get short-term disability, which prevented disciplinary action from my employer. A few weeks later Anthony called to apologize. He asked if he could come talk. I agreed. I needed some understanding. He apologized as he offered an explanation. He wanted to explain to me what I did wrong—I'd made him angry. He was excusing himself and blaming me for my black eye. He was sorry but he really wanted me to understand where he was coming from.

I wasn't at all satisfied but I married him and I had a child on the way. We needed to try again; he wasn't just a boyfriend I could walk away from. A few minutes after I agreed to give him another chance he told me he needed $5,000 to pay off his car. So you came back to get my income tax return? I was so disgusted but needed to m o v e forward. I paid off his car then tried to focus on my upcoming arrival.

Anthony started to make appointments with his psychiatrist. He admitted that not only did he have a psychiatrist, but he had been seeing him for two years. "For what?" I asked. I now started to understand, that what I had observed, were symptoms of a mental disorder. Why had he kept such an important thing from me? I would later learn that mental illness ran in his family heavily. Really? I am about to have a child with an unstable, abusive and unpredictable man.

His family, who I thought had it together, were certifiably crazy. Still, I didn't run. I realized, however, that I had to be even more understanding. OK, I'll take on this challenge as if I just learned my husband had cancer. I let him off the hook, mostly because he was not well. I looked at him with sympathy and tried to be supportive of his treatment. He became somber, gained weight and needed a push to go to work. He would withdraw from me and quickly get an attitude that would last weeks.

One day my water broke and I called my husband. He didn't answer. I called my sister Donna to take me to the hospital. I let Anthony's parents know what was going on, and just hoped that my husband would not ignore me through the birth of our son. Anthony and my mom were in the delivery room. Only two people were allowed in at a time.

Anthony's mother asked to come in. When she arrived she was drunk, and wasn't allowed to come in. So I avoided having to make her feel bad. I had a C-section, not because of any complications but I had requested C-sections since my first baby. Anthony named our son Shaquil, after the basketball player. When I returned home I was unable to function at one hundred percent; I was going to need my husband to help while I healed. Anthony would feed himself and leave me alone with our son. I had to remind him to fix me something to eat. Our issues worsened as I learned more and more disturbing things about my husband.

I found a receipt in his work bag for a hand gun that he'd purchased right before we got married. While we dated he never expressed any interest in owning a gun. I asked him, "Why in the world would you buy a gun a week before we get married? Were you going to mention that you had a gun?" I was relieved that he had not picked it up yet. I reminded him that we have small children and I refused to be in the same household with a gun. I don't think he ever picked it up.

Anthony was also addicted to porn. He brought from an apartment that he'd shared with his roommate a big bag full of porn. Not only did he continue to leave the bag open on my side of the closet, he sat it on top of my shoes because he didn't want to ruin his. When I'd come home from work I'd find my husband on the living room couch asleep to porn. I repeatedly explained that leaving that filth around was abusive to my children. He would laugh and say, "My bad," as if to say "No big deal." I realized that he didn't consider what I said of much importance.

I threw a birthday party for my older son Tayvon when he was turning 8. I had invited all of my friends to bring their children. Of course there would be cake and ice cream. I rented movies for the kids to watch in the living room. I turned on the TV and porn popped on the screen for every child and their parent to see. I was so hurt for these kids. It was bad enough that my children were exposed to this, now my friend's kids had to see this garbage?

Short of giving up, I didn't know what to do. I called the insurance company about getting marriage counseling. I had hoped that a professional could explain to Anthony what he was doing in a way he understood. They sent me to a therapist that authorized us to see a marriage counselor. We went to the same facility that Anthony went to for his depression.

This place had all kinds of mental health professionals, doctors and therapists. I told a doctor every reason that we needed therapy—that we were newly married and Anthony just wouldn't stop his destructive behavior. I waited for some optimism. The doctor stood up and said, "I will give you the referral, but it won't work." What, it won't work? He didn't even bother to elaborate. "So, it won't work," I thought, as I rode home feeling so bad. I didn't want this therapist to tell me that my marriage had no hope. I decided that when we saw the therapist I would take some of the blame. I took a more protective approach so that I wouldn't hear that we couldn't be helped.

We were referred to Ms. Margaret, a Jewish woman in her late 50's or early 60's. I didn't talk about the porn, instead I talked about what I did wrong. Anthony agreed, "Yeah, she really is a horrible wife." I wanted help but I wanted to ease into what he did wrong so he wouldn't feel attacked, and she wouldn't look at him as a lost cause. I continued to make appointments but Anthony decided he couldn't be bothered. I, however, kept going to therapy. If he didn't want to go that was fine, I was now in search of answers for me, and how I made such bad decisions. I ran away from bad and got worse. I started once a week. I focused mostly on myself and my family.

I told Anthony that he would need to take his porn with him when he left or keep it in his trunk. We decided to get a house. Anthony had quit school in his third year and now was making good money. He decided against being a lawyer; and said he'd keep being a laborer for the local steel company. I told him to keep going, even though I couldn't see him as a lawyer. He had no social or communication skills. He lacked basic common sense.

I had always paid for what I wanted up front so I had no credit. Anthony decided to get everything for us in his name. I didn't mind, since I knew I couldn't get a house on my own. The realtor showed us house after house then encouraged us to get a curbside view of houses on our own then report the ones we wanted to take a closer look at. We were approved for $150,000; that was good for our first home.

That would get us a modest single family home. We knew what we had to save and we started saving. I paid all the bills with my salary, and he agreed to save his entire checks. It was difficult. I no longer bought lunch; I didn't eat but I noticed my husband had new CDs and sneakers. I held up my side of the deal and kept going. It was a seller's market and nice houses would have multiple bids, so my realtor urged us to decide and then move fast. We went through the list and there were homes I just loved. But this one house I got such a bad vibe from. The neighbor's children looked evil, as if they'd never seen black people. And the house just gave me the creeps. I told Anthony we can look at every house but this one. I don't even want to look inside. That is how sure I was that I did not want to live there.

During the process my daughter Kacey, who was now 10, got a really bad stomach ache. I took her to the E.R. and several tests were run. The severity of her pain gave me great concern and she was admitted, so of course I stayed by her side. Anthony continued to look at houses without me. He called while I was in the hospital and said he found this house and it was wonderful but he needed to move quickly because there were several bids on it already.

He told me I would love it and asked if I trusted him to make the decision without me. I didn't, but I didn't much care about anything other than what was going on with my daughter. I agreed. When my daughter was released to come home Anthony and I, the realtor and Anthony's father went to see this home he and his parents had chosen. I couldn't believe it, driving up to this house that this was going to be our home.

My stomach was in knots. The only house with neighbors that gave me the creeps, the one house that I said I hated and didn't even want to look at was now my home. We looked at houses ten times better, but we end up with this one. I was disappointed and confused because I knew I was so clear. I again brushed it off, so we could move forward.

I looked at the bright side; we had a bigger home and were moving.

We went inside and I was still so very disappointed. Our bedroom was in the attic. In it was our personal bathroom with a hot tub. The kids' room was downstairs. They had ground-level windows and doors everywhere. I had small kids and what I didn't want was to be so far away from them. Anything could happen and I wouldn't hear a thing. Also, soon they would be teenagers and there were more than a few ways to sneak in and out of the house without being detected.

This was the worst house for someone with kids. His father commented, "Anthony, this house would be perfect for our assisted living residents." His parents, who were having financial problems because of their past mistakes ran an assisted living program out of their apartment. They only had one patient but desired to one day have a big enough space for more. I was so hurt. But I chose to again just get over it. Many nights I slept downstairs on the couch to be close to my kids.

The first week in the house I came home from work and Anthony is dressed in his best sports jersey. My attempt to make conversation was met by agitation. I handled him very carefully. I offered to make dinner, and he says angrily, "I just need some air." I said, "OK Captain." I sometimes wondered how he got into college, he was truly horrible with cover-ups. He came home late that night and says, "I have a surprise." I say, "OK." "I guess he isn't mad anymore," I think. He takes me by the hand and leads me outside and shows me this 2003 GMC, Yukon Denali. It was fully loaded, rims and all. I'm livid, I shout, "I know this isn't ours. Our children don't have beds, we have no money saved, and we just bought a house. Why would you get something so expensive without even consulting me?" He says, "I am the one paying for it with my money." I remind him, "You are not Lil Wayne. We don't have a video life-style. Our mortgage was $1,061 a month. His truck payments were $900 a month; the truck cost $72,000! How did he get a truck that expensive, he didn't even have a down payment?

They got him so good. Anthony worked four 12-hour shifts a week, 7 a.m. to 7 p.m. and 7p.m. to 7 a.m. I wanted our son to go to day care but he didn't want to pay for it so we sent our son to his mother, who was an alcoholic. I would be so worried. Not only was she a drunk, she had four humongous territorial cats that would scratch my newborn son's face and pee on his belongings. His mother, Mabel, would laugh and say her cats were just jealous because they were her babies. Shaquil would cry all night at the top of his lungs.

He wouldn't go to sleep unless I drove him around for an hour. But as soon as I brought him back in the house he was screaming at the top of his lungs again. Sometimes I went for days without sleeping. I would be so exhausted that I sometimes couldn't get out of bed. Then my daughter couldn't sleep. She was starting to stay up. It was as if we could get no peace in that house. Not sleeping would take its toll on me. I could go only so far on fumes.

CHAPTER 17

DAMAGED BEYOND RECOGNITION

THERE ARE SITUATIONS IN LIFE that can either make or break you. People are assigned to your life that will change you. One thing for certain was this: if I survived this experience I would be changed for the good. I was taking care of my colicky child, then having to go to work lethargic. No matter what shift Anthony was on I received no relief. The many nights that I forced myself to stay up with the baby changed my sleep pattern. Even when I was able to rest I couldn't.

I also worried heavily about my son and those aggressive, gigantic cats and the little care his grandmother gave him because of her drinking. I couldn't focus at work. Plus, I was having a hard time getting to work. I started to call out; the stress started to take such a toll that I spoke to my gynecologist and she prescribed Zoloft, an anti-depressant. I didn't see the benefits, I just felt like I was in a fog.

She recommended that I see a mental health specialist. I didn't have to travel far in my search, I knew where a factory of them were. I was still seeing my therapist Ms. Margaret. She walked me over to be seen by Dr. Monty—Anthony and his mom's psychiatrist.

Our first session was about 30 minutes. I described my symptoms: irritability, sadness and anger. He put me on a stronger anti-depressant, Effexor. The first two weeks on this medication I felt so loopy and foggy. Dr. Monty prescribed me time off of work, so that I could get the medication in my system. I started seeing images of someone touching me as a little girl. I couldn't make out whom it was, but then I would see my dad's face right after that. I was so confused and scared.

I didn't know what I was seeing and from how long ago. I didn't know if I was reliving something that actually happened or was I piecing together flashbacks of several situations. I wasn't sure but I knew I wanted off of these meds. When I went back in to see Dr. Monty, Anthony went first to talk to him. When Dr. Monty saw me he was cold; he told Anthony to make me do stuff around the house. I ignored the comment and the disdain in his eyes. I then told him what I had been experiencing.

Dr. Monty diagnosed me with bipolar disorder. I didn't know much about it but I was relieved that I was now going to get treatment that would help me; after all, I still wasn't sleeping. Our session only lasted about five minutes. I assumed that since he talked to my husband before me he didn't need to see me long. And now I had a host of medications that I needed to take regularly that my doctor had prescribed. I trusted him. I just wanted a sense of normalcy and I was determined to get better. The first few weeks on this medication my symptoms were worse than they were when I took Effexor. I now had a slew of side effects that had me in a zombie-like state. I took three medications instead of one, one of which was an anti-psychotic. I asked my husband what he thought, since he had more information about this medication stuff. He insisted that I needed to keep taking them for a while before I would feel better. He assured me that most medication is prescribed for a multitude of illnesses, and that they don't just give anti-psychotic medication to you simply because you're psychotic. So I trusted what I was told.

One day my husband came to me and said, "You don't have to go back to work if you don't want to." I was in shock; we had responsibilities. What about our bills and his truck payment? I was impressed because it was rare to see my husband so caring. I was still so tired, now I was medicated and still unable to rest. Every trip back to the doctors meant an increase in and or switch of medications.

My doctor advised me to stick with it and assured me that this was a process of getting the correct dosage levels. I told him I am getting worse with all the side effects. I continued to have insomnia so Dr. Monty gave me a two-week sample of a medication called Zyprexa, an anti-psychotic drug used to medicate people suffering from schizophrenia and bipolar disorder. In two weeks I went from 160 lbs. to 180.

My husband was angry at me, again. I didn't know why and, because of my new meds, I didn't care. He was back over his parents' house but I needed him to come get the baby as advised by my doctor. I was on the couch watching TV, that is, it was watching me because I could barely focus. Something about this irritated him; he went to the kitchen, slammed the cabinets and threw dishes on the floor. I continued to look at TV. I called my mom to come get my son.

Anthony stormed into the living room and hurled a canned good through the 60-inch TV screen that he'd purchased. I didn't take my eyes off the screen. By now my mom had arrived, thank God, because my son still was crawling around on the floor all while Anthony was throwing a temper tantrum. I didn't respond, so it made him even angrier. When my mom came he grabbed our son so she couldn't get him. I took my meds and was out in ten minutes.

His tantrums seemed more frequent and over the top when I was under medication. He was back and forth to my doctor but wasn't receiving any treatment. I now suspect that my husband was telling all kinds of horrific stories about me so that the doctor would keep increasing my dosage. I stayed so out of it, but I fought to hold on to my responsibilities.

My desire to get better kept me in the psychiatrist's office. I saw my therapist two times a week; still, I was too embarrassed to tell the truth about my husband's abusive behavior. I feared that I would be told to leave him. My meds increased and switched so rapidly that I was never even able to finish a whole bottle.

I saw signs, even before being drugged, that my husband was cheating. I turned a blind eye to it, though, since I had no proof and didn't really want to know for sure. I blamed a lot of my husband's behavior on his children's mother who wouldn't let him see his daughters. And since I was home so much, I decided to search for them. I thought it would be difficult to find them but it wasn't. I got a name from Anthony's mom and got a hold of the children's grandmother, who said Anthony doesn't want to pay child support, to which I replied, "No, he won't mind at all."

I pleaded with her to have the mother of his children call him, so he could be a part of his children's lives. I was so excited to share the awesome news with him. I just knew this would bring him peace and stop all of his bad behavior. When I told him he shouted, "You are so stupid! Now we have to pay child support!" I was appalled. To think I actually believed this man really wanted a relationship with his daughters.

Knowing he really had no excuse for being such an explosive jerk caused me to face a truth that I wasn't prepared for. His daughter's mother started calling him at inappropriate times of the night and they would talk for hours. He started to disappear again. He was nice to her and promised he would pay $500 a month. She was so happy. She didn't know this was a ploy to keep her from filing in the courts where she would have been awarded almost double. Once again I got a clearer view of this man.

I remember him telling me, before we were married, that he was fooling around with this girl who later tried to say her son was his, but that she was lying because she thought he was a catch. I advised him to get a DNA test, but when he changed his number and just moved on I stopped bringing it up. Later I considered the child, who was fatherless, and a mother that was abandoned by a selfish, self-centered man who felt no attachment to his children.

Anthony's disrespect of me continued. Signs of cheating were so blatant. I believe he *wanted* me to know. One day a cellphone rang. Since neither of us had cellphones, I got up to see why this sound was coming from his pants. He dove on me and started to wrestle me. It was obvious that he had a cellphone now, even though I was unaware that he had one before then.

The fact that he was more concerned about the caller left me devastated. He agreed that if I wouldn't answer his phone he would tell me everything. He told me that he had a cellphone, which was obvious. That he purchased two, one for him and one for his employee. He said that since things were so tight he decided to get into selling marijuana and he had a girl selling for him so he bought a family cell- phone plan so he could reach her.

I hit him with a snow scraper and tried to cry but no tears came. I believe it was a symptom of the meds. I was so hurt. I couldn't handle all the stress. I decided that I was leaving and filed for divorce. I couldn't focus, so I never went back to court to take any of the other steps. When the process was explained to me the words went in one ear and came out the other. I knew Anthony would make it so difficult for me and I thought I wasn't strong enough mentally to fight him. How could I leave, where was I going?

I'd been diagnosed with bipolar disorder, an emotional disease that caused instability in your moods—one would be so full of energy that they would stay up for days then crash into depression. The sufferer could experience extreme anger, for no reason. Bipolar, so they say, is also hereditary. Most of the times his mother and I had the same medication. I so wanted to escape.

My concentration was horrible. I had to stay on the medication because if I stopped cold turkey I would plummet into a suicidal depression, which I learned the hard way. I felt trapped. My intention was to continue with my doctor and therapist because, after all this time and different medications, they have to be close to getting it right so I could get back to work and leave this man. Until then I was trapped inside my own mind not even able to communicate. I was so forgetful and still unable to sleep without my legal drugs.

My eldest son Tayvon, at 9, had become such a problem. One day I was attempting to discipline him when he started fighting me back. I couldn't handle him without getting dizzy. So for the first time, out of desperation, I allowed my husband to physically step in. Anthony went in Tayvon's room and shut the door behind him. I could hear him hitting my son. I never wanted anyone to physically discipline my children but me, but I didn't know what to do with him. I was sure that if he thought he could overpower me and felt I was no threat this could lead to greater problems from him. I stayed at the door, and with pain in my heart for my son, I tried to let Anthony finish but he kept beating and beating him. Finally I busted through the door to find my son with a big bloody gash on his face. He must have been hitting him like my stepfather hit us, anywhere. And even when he drew blood, he had no intentions of stopping. I gathered my kids and went to my sister Arlene's house. I felt like I had just done what I promised I would never do to my kids. That was it! I needed to protect us, but how?

My family wasn't positioned to take us in indefinitely. I was under doctors' care and on short-term disability, and nowhere near getting better. I stayed at Arlene's for about two weeks. Anthony called me wanting to talk. I met him at the house to find the lights cut off. He didn't resent me, but he wanted to tell me that I couldn't move back in with my kids and have electricity without him, so I needed to make a decision. I was so disgusted I wanted so badly to get up and walk away. But I couldn't even take care of myself or hold a job, thanks to this bipolar disorder the doctor said I had.

How long would it be before they could find the right medication? I must have the most complex case of bipolar ever. My search for treatment left me in worse condition than when I began. I agreed to take him back, and even though I wanted to report him to the authorities for what he did to my son I weighed my options. What would I do then? He was the one with the income. Life became increasingly difficult. During the summer Anthony would work out for hours nonstop, wouldn't eat or sleep, then disappear. He was tired, irritable, argumentative and aggressive. He was still leaving porn around the house for my kids to find, something he made no apologies for. While on leave, my job let me go. I fought for the disability that my job provided. The decision was overturned after six months. After that, I would need to apply for Social Security.

Now with my own income I had a little more flexibility, but still not enough to leave. I bought my kids an inexpensive computer for school. Anthony had visited so many porn sites before they even used it that every time they turned it on images of people having sex would pop up. I was so over him. I set a goal to get out of this marriage even though I wasn't sleeping and had trouble focusing. I *had* to figure this out.

Summer came and Anthony's mom had another one of her drunken, manic episodes. She claimed she wanted to cut herself, and that she wanted to die. I drove her to the emergency room, just as I had driven her to her appointments, the store and anywhere else she needed to go. She needed to resume her medication. When she took herself off, she plummeted into a suicidal depression—one of the side effects of coming off of the medication abruptly.

In October Anthony threw another tantrum and resumed his pattern of leaving the house for long periods of time. I figured he'd gotten a new girlfriend. I started my search. I looked through the computer history and found an online dating site. I pulled up the email that I'd helped him set up and found details of his communications with women he had agreed to meet. I knew it! These tantrums were just smoke and mirrors, a way for him to live the single life while I was trapped in this marriage and house. One day I called him, to ask him to come over. He came. I showed him my evidence. He didn't say a word. He didn't even care that I found it. I became enraged and slapped him. I wanted a response. I got a response, too. But not the one I was at all expecting. He called the cops on me.

When they showed up he calmly said, "My wife is bipolar and violent, I pay all the bills and she doesn't work." I tried to tell my version of what happened, and couldn't get a complete, coherent sentence out. Only ramblings emerged from my mouth because I could not believe this man was having me arrested. The police handcuffed me, and he didn't show one emotion...as if I was no more than a bag of garbage.

Handcuffed and stripped and told to cough while squatting, I felt so humiliated and hurt by my husband's infidelity, but mostly by his callous attitude toward having me arrested. I was devastated beyond words. I was in jail for three days before my sister bailed me out. I told the jail staff about my medication; by the time they were ready to give it to me I was going home. I caught a cab home, smelly and feeling lower than I had ever felt in my life. I felt like I had made a mistake that I couldn't recover from.

The worse part was the loss of my daughter's respect for me. She asked me, "Why do you let him do these things to you and stay?" My response was, "It's complicated." She gave me the same look that I'd given my mother when I was her age, the look of disgust and embarrassment. How did I get here? I'd promised I would never walk in these shoes. I felt worthless and unlovable. It occurred to me that even my kids would be better off without me. My own husband hates me, and every time my toddler returned to me from my in-laws, someone had taught him to say, "Mommy is a F@#% up." I just wanted to sleep and not wake up. I didn't resume the medications; I didn't want to have to go deal with those terrible side effects waiting for it to get in my system. Soon I was planning my forever exit.

My kids were at school. I called Anthony to tell him that I was no longer going to be his problem. I wrote a suicide note to let my mom know I loved her and to assure my kids that it wasn't their fault. I had been on so many medications that I had a shopping bag full of half full bottles. I took them all. My kids had a half-day and as they were approaching the house they saw my husband simulate knocking on the door.

Later, my daughter said she was wondering why he was pretending to knock. Then, she said, he jumped back in his car. He never saw them. They came in the house and went to their rooms. A while later my mom shows up. The crazy thing about this was that she never pops up; she should have been at work. The kids let her in. She calls me downstairs. I'm still alert, so I go. She asked to use my bathroom. I remember trying to look normal and telling her to use the main one downstairs. She says, "I want to use yours." She goes upstairs and finds my note. By the time she gets back downstairs I am unconscious. I never even knew my kids were home. My mom tells them what medications I had taken.

The ambulance rushed me to the nearest hospital. My mother wasn't allowed to go because they didn't think I would make it. They told her I was in pretty bad condition. When she got to the hospital the medics still had not brought me in because they were still trying to resuscitate me. When I finally arrived they told my mom that I wasn't out of the woods just yet, and even if I survived there would be severe lasting effects.

When I woke up I had a bunch of tubes down my throat and nose. I was angry that I was still alive. I yanked every tube out. A nurse says to me," You know you are pretty lucky." I rolled my eyes. Luck had nothing to do with it. I knew I shouldn't be here. Why didn't it work? The heartache was too much to deal with.

I learned my sister thought I was being a drama queen. Did *anyone* love me? Did I have any purpose? I was moved to a more permanent room. There I saw a familiar face, my mom's childhood friend, nurse Nancy. She gave me a book, *The Purpose Driven Life*. I couldn't care less about a book or a sermon. My pain was so intense I couldn't see how I was going to make it another day. Nothing anyone could give me could provide the relief I craved. "Nurse, you want to help me? Tell me where I can go smoke a cigarette."

CHAPTER 18

BENT BUT NOT BROKEN

AFTER A SUICIDE ATTEMPT they make you stay in the hospital psych ward. I stayed three days, painting trinkets and sitting in groups. The doctor on staff lowered the dosage of my medication. I returned to the loveless home that reminded me of all my pain. I would take long baths as an escape. Only my bedroom was upstairs. My master bathroom had a hot tub. I would stay in the tub for hours, daydreaming of a better life. I would escape in my daydreams.

In my dream I would be in a beautiful new house with my new husband. Anthony would have to visit his son. When he'd knock on our door, we were always laughing. My new husband and I were so in love. At that point I had nothing to compare it to, but it felt so real I didn't want the dream to end.

The most amazing thing started to happen in my daydreams. I started seeing myself in front of large audiences speaking to them in this voice that was bold and confident. The things I would say were wise and profound. I would attempt to write them down but by the time my hand was put to paper it all got fuzzy. My day dreamed version of me said some amazing things to uplift and inspire. What I heard myself say couldn't just be a daydream because I had wisdom. I thought maybe it was a glimpse of what my life would have looked like, had I not made such a mess of it.

I could barely communicate. I often wondered if I'd ever recover my concentration. Whenever sadness overcame me I'd take a long bath and escaped my painful reality. Anthony continued to be the back and forth husband. One moment he hated me, the other he loved me. I was so emotionally battered that when he wasn't cruel it felt like we were on our honeymoon. His bouts of remorsefulness would not last very long. It was never more than two months before he had found someone new and sought to destroy me. When my long-term disability ran out I was back to solely depending on him. I often went without basic necessities.

Unless he was in a good mood, I couldn't even ask him for groceries. I had a toothache for months. It was unbearable. I would cry, and even though we had insurance he would not pay the copay for me to see a dentist. The toothache affected my whole body. Finally, after suffering and crying for months, Anthony agreed to send me to the dentist. By then I needed a root canal. The dentist started the work, but when I was supposed to return Anthony was back to hating me so I never got the cap put on.

He refused to give me the second payment; he told me it was my problem. He met someone new and was out the door. I asked him to return. He said he didn't love me like a wife, and the other woman had goals. At this point everyone could see I needed to leave but I was not feeling like I had any worth or options. My best friend Alisha accompanied me to the psychiatrist. She wanted to show him that he had made a mistake, to assure him that I wasn't crazy— my husband was. I looked at Alisha with pity, because she couldn't accept the truth. I *was* bipolar and my doctor was just trying to help me. I wasn't as foggy, because my dosage had been reduced and I'd switched doctors.

I had to be crazy, I would load clothes into the washing machine, go back to retrieve them and nothing was in there. I was always losing clothes that I had laid out. I had no underwear. I couldn't understand where I was putting these things, and how I kept forgetting time or where our clothes were going. Whenever I started to feel better I could rely on Anthony to attack me.

One evening I was home with my son when Anthony, his mother, father and neighbor showed up at my door. They took my son from me, out of the house covered with nothing but a blanket. He was otherwise naked. I called my stepdad and mother, and they came. When they showed up, Anthony's father was pushing me, as I struggled to get my 2-year-old son out of the car.

My stepfather demanded that they let go of my son and they did and sped off. What kind of explanation did this man give that convinced three old people to be despicable? The reality was that they made their share of mistakes parenting Anthony; he was exposed to a lot. And sadly they supported him and his craziness. Nothing he did was his fault or wrong. I had no peace. When I'd drift off I would sometimes find Anthony standing over me. I was so used to not sleeping that sometimes I would have insomnia for two weeks, but I was still functioning. I went to therapy and the therapist advised that I needed to admit myself into the hospital because not sleeping was dangerous. So I finished up with the kids, got them settled at my sisters, and admitted myself.

I was so uptight that the medication had to be increased. When I went outside to smoke, I passed out outside. It became nearly impossible to induce rest, so I entered a sleep study. Meanwhile, my daughter Kacey was also experiencing the same type of restlessness; so she too was sent to a sleep study. No matter how many tests were administered, nothing explained my insomnia. I started to wean myself off of the medication and noticed how much better I felt.

However, I was careful. I didn't want to fall into a suicidal depression again. I was careful not to tell my therapist and doctor because they would try to terrify me with stories about me running naked through the streets if I stopped taking the meds. I was starting to lose trust in their professional opinion. I started to feel better so I enrolled in a class for refinancing and home insurance loans. Anthony was trying to get a loan against the house, and the woman that came to do the estimate of our home talked to me about the classes.

I was feeling hopeful about completing the class since I was no longer on so much medication. I was able to concentrate better, not perfect, but much better. I didn't allow her to complete the loan application but I paid my deposit to complete the training course. I knew I had to do something to escape this situation. Or I would have stay depending on Anthony.

One evening I went to get Shaquil from Anthony's. Anthony attempted to take the tags off the car, since the car was in his name. He knew I needed this car in order to complete my classes. I took my son and sped off. I continued moving forward with my classes. One day I got a call from Anthony. He wanted to tell me he'd done something that he regretted. He went to court and got a warrant for my arrest. He claimed I'd attempted to hit him with a car.

I knew he was just attempting to thwart my progress, so that I would have to be dependent upon him. It always amazed me how hard he tried to destroy me, how he did not want me, and yet he couldn't stand the thought of me being free. I called then turned myself in. The cops told me they didn't believe him, that when they spoke to him he hadn't even gone to the hospital, that he wasn't limping nor in any pain as far as they could see. Still, because the claim was made they had to arrest me. Again I got to spend three days in jail for attempting to take a class to better mine and my children's lives.

I was tired, but I was no longer just sad, I was angry. I wasn't going to continue to be his victim and this wasn't going to end unless I stopped it. I continued with my therapy; I even went to the psychiatrist. When I was prescribed medication I neglected to take it. One visit to Margaret, I was calm and collected and even losing the medication weight. "It is odd for someone who is b i p o l a r to consistently come to therapy as you do," she says, "because usually when you're bipolar you have these manic times when you feel so good that you don't follow doctor's orders, so it's hard to have a consistent bipolar patient." She added, "I wonder if it is in fact your husband who is bipolar?" I wanted so badly to say, "You think!" But I no longer needed her validation or cared about her opinion. I continued therapy because I was committed to understanding myself better.

My mother dealt with an abuser. My grandmother dealt with an abuser. Now I am dealing with an abuser. I want the cycle to end. I was still desperate and hungry for change and so determined to not let this man destroy me. I didn't know how I was going to stop this but it had to stop with me. I never wanted my daughter to go through this. I may have stayed too long but if she does experience this, I'm going to learn some things that I'll be able to teach her. This curse has to be broken. I sought help from the pastors at our church.

I remember speaking to our associate pastor, Raye. I told him that I was diagnosed with bipolar disorder; that I often battled with depression, and that I didn't seem to have control over my moods. I frequently felt weighed down. He told me that it was not bipolar, that I was under a generational curse. I didn't understand what he meant by that but I knew I wanted to understand. I spoke with our new senior pastor, Frank Rupert, and I told him I needed prayer and that I couldn't fight this by myself.

He told me to come back on Wednesday at 6, to his office, he'll be there waiting for me. I felt such anticipation, because it felt like I was finally connecting with the right people. I wanted to call Pastor Rupert but I could not move. It was as if this heavy, invisible cloak was draped over me and the more I wanted to get up and go the more guilt and feelings of oppression overtook me. I was not dealing with just emotions; I was dealing with something though invisible was real—a heavy, dark spirit.

I kept pushing forward. I started to wake up early in the morning, about 4:30 or 5. I heard this voice small and still whisper, "Just take a walk. Clear your head." That really helped. I would take these long walks while it was still dark out, and I would talk with God. The fog was lifting.

It became more and more difficult for Anthony to move me; he tried crying for me to love him. He even visited my church and answered an altar call. I rolled my eyes because I knew it was his desperate attempt to get me back under his control. He was unsuccessful no matter what he tried. He walked in one day in tears and asked, "Can we pray together?" Frustrated, I screamed, "Lord God, let this man leave me alone!" One day I got a call from him saying he was going to jump off a bridge. Skeptical, but not willing to risk it after all I knew now, I took him to my once psychiatrist, Dr. Monty. I told him that Anthony was threatening to kill himself. The doctor asked him was he in fact thinking of harming himself? Anthony said, "Yes."

The look on this doctor's face was priceless. He had been busy listening to my abuser's updates on how psycho I was, when in fact the patient that you'd been treating for years was actually showing signs of instability all along. He called the Psych Ward and that day Anthony was committed. And he went willingly. Every day I visited him he would yell at the nurses. He was a very difficult patient; exhibiting behaviors you would probably see from a psychotic patient.

Traumatic experiences continued during this time. I met my brother Kevin. He was a son that my father had approximately 19 years earlier. I was excited to meet him, and I went right into treating him like a little brother. He moved in with my sister Arlene. Anthony was now back at home and when he went to work I let my brother drive his truck. It was fun having him around.

Also during this time I cracked the voicemail codes on my husband's phone and learned that he was once again having an affair. On the other end of the line I heard a thick accented African woman saying she missed her appointment and it was too late. I learned her phone number and called her. It was what I suspected. She was pregnant and too far along to abort. He had taken her to the appointment but she was explaining to him that she had no other place to go for no one would take her that late in her pregnancy. Devastated and again humiliated I also learned that she didn't even know his real name or where he worked.

I made sure she had all of that information when I spoke with her. I gave her his social security number, his real name and his work number. I gave her my information and told her to reach me when she had the baby and I would make sure that he took responsibility for his child. I asked her how far along she was? I was amazed to hear how far she was because she'd gotten pregnant about the time my husband falsely accused me of hitting him with a car and had me arrested. She lived right down the street. So, did Anthony get me arrested to freely cheat on me down the street with a woman in our neighborhood? The craziest thing was that prior to him having me arrested he'd just cried and pleaded to come back home. He assured me that he'll never do it again and even went and got my name tattooed on his arm—my name is eight letters long and he'd never had a tattoo before. This is what he thought would convince me that he would never cheat again. I didn't believe him for a second, that a tattoo was proof that he'd be faithful. But I did find the whole matter amusing.

So he is having a child with another woman during our marriage. This was as good as it could get for me, as stressed out as I had been. I'd been humiliated before, but this truly took the cake. Later that same year my sister and her husband had a domestic dispute. It was pretty serious, my daughter needed to pry them apart. Her husband was about to be deployed and he attacked my sister. When I got there my sister's face was a bloody mess; if my daughter were not there she probably would not have made it.

Around this time I had taken the vehicle; when Anthony had been in a cheerful mood I'd convinced him to sign it over to me. Even though I couldn't register it because I had no license, my sister agreed to put it in her name. We so badly wanted her to leave her husband, for her safety. Soon after this attack my little brother Kevin was shot and killed.

During this time my sister took her husband back and wanted us to forget that he tried to kill her. Having lost one sibling it made me even more determined to make sure I showed up in court to bring my daughter as a witness. My sister didn't want to risk her husband going to jail, and she became very angry with me. They would sometimes drive past my house.

One night they took the tags that were registered to my sister off my car and threatened that if I didn't leave matters alone that she was going to claim my car as her own. We managed. We caught cabs or got rides. Every court date we showed up to testify. He was military, so his lawyers kept postponing the case. They were hoping to wear us out. Eight hours a day we waited in the courthouse waiting room. On August 21, 2006, a month after my brother was killed, Anthony decided to show up with us for court and wait with us. He was never supportive. I had no idea what he was up to. Again, the case was postponed. We returned home.

My stepsister and I were on the couch grieving for my brother Kevin. We had been reading the word of God together, trying to find words of solace. We were not perfect; we were smoking cigarettes while reading. Still, we needed a word from God to gain some understanding of all that was happening all around us. Anthony no longer stayed with me. When he visited, it would mostly be to harass me. He would come by occasionally, which I couldn't stop because it was his home as well. While I was grieving and my sister and brother-in-law attacked me, I believe he thought that this was a perfect time for me to fall apart and maybe end back up on medication. He came downstairs. I could always tell when he was under the influence of a dark spirit because his eyes changed and he'd have this growl about his mouth. It's hard to describe, but in fact I could sense from his countenance that he was about to attack before he even spoke a word. He walked over and snatched my cigarette out of my hand. I leapt up and said, "Why do you always have to do something?" He runs to the phone laughing and does this childish type dance. Then he calls 911 and says, "My wife just hit me with her shoe." No, I'm not scared this time. I'm not on medication. My mind is stronger. I'm not going to be an anxious mess, either.

Besides, I have a witness—my stepsister. I knew I wasn't going to jail. When the police arrived I stayed calm. Anthony goes into his spiel about me being bipolar and violent, lying that I hit him with my shoe. The police officer asked if I had hit him. Anthony pointed to his pocket, which was directly where his wallet was. The cop wrote that in the report. The cop asked me what happened. I said, "Officer, I have done nothing to this man." The officer turns to my stepsister and says, "Did you see what happened?" She had such an anxiety for cops she said, "I didn't see anything."

I could not believe it. My only witness to what just happened isn't standing up for me and telling the officer what really happened. He then asked me to stand up and put my hands behind my head, and then he put cuffs on me. Tears started to roll down my cheeks; this is not fair. It was at that very moment that I realized with all of the warfare that I had been experiencing it wasn't because I was on medication, it wasn't even about my diagnosis, but the devil had been after me. He exposed himself that day. As the cops handcuffed me in tears I said, "Father, forgive them." I understood that this was not an attack of the physical but this was a spiritual attack. God must have a greater plan for my life. I didn't know how but I was determined to fight back.

This was a hard month; the warfare continued. Me, my sisters and all our children went out to Patterson Park to swim. We heard gunshots. We all scrambled to pile into a car. Then we saw a cop shooting in our direction. A cop, standing in front of this car that is full of women and children, commands us to get out and sit on the curb. Now, the suspects were black men who were running in the opposite direction.

The cop was white and bald with flames of fire tattooed on his arm; he looked like a skinhead. This cop put us all in cuffs in front of our children and ordered us to the curb. My step- sister started crying. I looked at the cop, and said to her, "Do not cry, I'm getting his badge number." He looked at my ID and address. Then he took the handcuffs off of me and said, "You can go now." I told him I wasn't leaving without my sisters. My father shows up to see what was going on with us. They take my youngest sister and him to jail with the ridiculous trumped up charge that they were running from the cops yelling "f*** the police".

My youngest sister has never been to jail. She's never committed a crime. I wish I could say the same about my father, but he was no longer a career criminal. He just showed up to see about his daughters. Not surprisingly, the matter was thrown out of court without it being heard. I suspected that this cop had a history of such offenses. The enemy was sending attack after attack; we hadn't even gotten a full month past the death of my brother and it was as if a message to put me back under the rock of depression went out. I had been in cuffs enough to not be moved or intimidated.

We were trying to spend more time as a family. A month after I lost my brother, my family is harassed by cops. My sister and her husband are harassing me, and threaten to take my car from me. My husband has me arrested for no reason, again. I was determined not to give up. I must be getting closer!

CHAPTER 19

GIVE UP OR SURRENDER

THREE MORE DAYS IN JAIL but this time I was at peace. I wasn't afraid and I wasn't even angry. I had this feeling that everything was going to be fine. It was at that time when it was so clear that I was in a fight but not with Anthony. This was a spiritual battle and if I was such a target then I must be more important than I thought. I had this awakening, that this was the devil attacking. I must have a great assignment. In jail I had this peace that I was able to pass on. I was encouraging women in my cell. I was even praying for them. One woman said, "You don't even belong here, you should be mad." I wasn't. I didn't know how but I knew without a doubt things would get better.

When I came back to the house, it had been wrecked. Nothing new. All my clothes were gone. I didn't even have a toothbrush. My kids' clothes were gone, even my son Shaquil, who was both of ours, had no clothes. Anthony took their toys and dumped trash all over the floor. The furniture was torn and mostly ruined. I left the home and stayed at my dad's. My mom bought us toothbrushes and underwear. It was two weeks before school would start and I had $42 in my account and needed to not only get school supplies but our basic necessities. I felt discouragement creeping in. There was that small still voice reminding me that I was not helpless or hopeless and that my power was in my prayer.

"Father, I don't know how you're going to fix this but Lord God I know that I do not want to continue on this path. You know that I stand in need. I need you to turn this situation around. I am not a victim and I will survive Lord. Show me what it is that you need from me. My kids start school soon. I have no money. I have no income. But what I know is that You are able to make a way, to turn it around. Please Lord, I am desperate. Savior, save me."

My mom went through the things that she had and we got the basic necessities: a couple of pens, a couple of notebooks, she even bought a few things so they would have an outfit to start school. It was far from everything that I needed but it would do. I would periodically go home to check the mail. During this time I received a letter from Social Security. I had been waiting for three years to hear something. Usually when you wait on a Social Security appeal decision, you get a letter indicating your court date so that you can appear in court and go before a judge.

The judge would then determine whether you were okay or still disabled and unable to work because of your medical condition. God had delivered me from thinking I needed to take medication. I was now thinking and speaking a lot clearer and no longer had symptoms of severe depression. I opened the letter to find not a court date but a ruling. I had been approved. Not only was I approved but they were going to pay me for the past three years that I had had no income. And I would be getting a check for several thousands of dollars.

Even though I was coming out, I still was unable to sleep. I still was unable to keep a job because of the trauma. My God had done it. He didn't even have me go through the usual process of having to explain why I no longer took the medication. My first installment would be coming shortly, $1,800—which was like a million to me. It seemed to have arrived in less than two weeks. I now had the money I needed to buy clothes and school supplies! The money was broken up in payments.

I struggled for so long, even without food. I even had to ask for the change out of my girlfriend's car to get two packs of Oodles of Noodles because Anthony refused to help. God saw what was happening and stepped in, in a supernatural way. I started with getting a new wardrobe for all of us. I purchased new furniture and painted all of the walls. Rather than have my father install new locks, I had him replace the whole door. I was determined to have peace. I was feeling so much stronger and renewed, and for the first time decorated my children's rooms and the house the way I wanted. Anthony had done so much destruction to our home.

Anthony would come home and track his dirty boots across our white bedroom floor. Looking back, I know why, he wanted to make sure that our bedroom was off limits to anyone else. But I scrubbed the carpet down and I bought a new computer and printer. Things are truly looking up after all of that heartache, and after all of the work that I had done on my own I turned around and saw my home looking more beautiful than it had ever looked. I remembered that I had citations in Virginia that I needed to take care of in order to restore my driver's license. I was nervous because it had been several years since I had heard anything about the tickets that I had left. I called the DMV and got a balance from Hampton and Newport News for all of the speeding tickets and violations that I had accumulated. The total was $10,000, but I knew I needed to clean that up.

The next month I was able to walk into the MVA with a reinstated Virginia license, as if I had never lost it, and get a Maryland driver's license for the first time. That meant so much to me, that I was moving forward, that I was now going to be legal. I could now register my car myself, legally, and no one could take it away from me. That Christmas, the Christmas tree was full of gifts for each one of my children. The decorations were so beautiful and my home finally looked like a home.

I soon worked on getting in school. It would be my first college experience. I enrolled in Baltimore City Community College. I took four courses: psychology, sociology, an Internet course, and dance aerobics. I was praying so much and I was hearing the voice of God directing my footsteps. The semester came and I really enjoyed school.

When the professor would ask questions I was the first to have my hand up. Some assignments that others struggled with, I turned in with confidence knowing that I had gotten an A. For someone that had been told that they were stupid for so long I discovered that I was actually quite intelligent. The aerobics helped me to stay in shape, and helped me lose the weight that those steroids and medication caused me to gain. My goal was to get some normalcy, to get back what had been taken from me.

I continued my journaling, began going to church and sought counsel consistently. I could see the envy in Anthony's eyes. He would come by to pick up Shaquil and accidentally, so he would say, knock over things like my stereo and break it. He hated that I was getting better. I was still in counseling at the time, still seeing Margaret, when he volunteered to go with me. I was suspicious. When we got there he was quick to tell her, "She's not on her medicine anymore."

He wasn't being supportive; he wanted someone to help him get me back on medication so he could regain control over me. It wasn't going to happen. At the end of my first semester, I had all A's. My goal at the time was to be a registered nurse. I knew that it would be hard work but I knew I could do it. I enrolled into the next semester, this time increasing the difficulty of courses. It wasn't very long before disaster would strike again.

All of the mortgage bills were sent to Anthony's parents' home, where he was staying. Since the home was in Anthony's name he was responsible for making sure the mortgage was paid. He never let me see the bills, he never told me when they were due. Right before the semester began our lights were cut off. I called Anthony and asked what happened. "What do you mean what happened? The bill hasn't been paid in months," he answered. I asked, "Why didn't you tell me that there was a balance, I would have paid it?" I'd feared that if I paid the bill he could have the electricity turned off to punish me. I needed to get them in my name so I would no longer have to rely on him. He said the balance was $3,500. I screamed, "You said you were paying the bills, I could've paid it when I had the money!" Even though they were in his name, he didn't seem to be worried about them at all. He was satisfied with making me suffer.

I quickly turned the lights back on illegally until I could figure out what to do. Less than a month later someone calls the company and tells them that my lights were on; they come back out and turn it back off, this time cutting me from the pole. I took some electric tape, climbed the roof and turned the lights back on. Shortly after the lights were cut off again. I didn't have $3,500 any longer. Neither was I feeling confident about paying bills that were not in my name because Anthony would only get them cut off again. He wasn't obligated to keep anything on, given that everything was in his name.

He had the lights cut off before even though they weren't past due, just to control me. I had a decision to make. With all the work that I had done on this home I was never going to be peaceful in it as long as it was in Anthony's name. It belonged to him. He had full access to harass and hurt us. My children and I were forced to go and stay with my sister who lived in a worse
part of town in a

small apartment with her three children. She only had room for a couple of bags of clothes and my computer. I took my computer system with me because I needed it for school. School was my way out. This was my plan A and B.

School started and I was determined to stay in. Occasionally I would have to go back to the house to get something that the kids or I needed. I once went home to find a man in my bedroom going through my things. I was angry. I asked, "Who are you and where did you come from?"

"The homeowner gave me permission to come here and evaluate the home because he's trying to sell it." I was livid. He was trying to sell our home out from underneath us. I knew I couldn't stop it and that before the courts could decide on how things ought to be settled, he could do whatever he wanted to. Another time I came home and found that he had given access to immigrant workers. All that was there were the kids' and my belongings, the only furnishing that he really owned was a new big screen TV that he had recently purchased.

I tried to get help with the bill from various agencies but because it wasn't in my name there was nothing anyone could do. BG&E, as long as there was a balance, would not let me switch the service into my name. Keeping up with my schoolwork was getting harder. My concentration was off. I couldn't focus on the assignments.

My income was $1,300 a month—not hardly enough to make rent, pay BG&E and still afford to keep my kids in a halfway decent neighborhood; honestly, it wasn't enough to get us in the worst of areas. Divorce papers that I had filed a year earlier, which I never followed up on, were reinstated. I was able to just reinstate it and wait for a court date. I filed for child support. We both had hearings that required us to go before a child support agent who would give us an amount that we would have to agree upon that was $462, which Anthony would have to pay monthly. He said he refused to pay it.

I pleaded with him. "You know I have to move," I said, "And I do not have enough income to move." "You're not getting a dime," he yelled. Since he wouldn't agree the matter had to be sent to the courts for a judge to make a ruling. That could take anywhere from six months to a year. After that hearing, outside I told Anthony that he wasn't going to get away with all he was doing to me. With this smug look on his face he calmly said, "I don't care."

Then he added, "You know what's so funny. I can bend you, but I just can't seem to break you." I stared at him with the most puzzled look. So you knew what you were doing the whole time, you had every intention to break me, to push me into a place of no return. I told him that this was going to come back on him. I returned to my sister's house feeling overwhelmed not knowing what to do. We couldn't possibly stay here but I didn't have enough to move.

My only option was to grovel and plead with Anthony to give us some type of assistance. I asked him to meet me at the house. I tried to talk to him, to reason with him. I explained that we didn't have to separate on such ugly terms and he needed to consider his son. We were actually getting along. Then he said, "This is really goodbye." Then he takes my son and runs out the door with him. It was a cool October night when he snatched Shaquil out of my hands and ran out the door with him coatless.

I called my mom and stepdad to come and help find them. We called the police and went to his parents' house; they said they hadn't seen him. We drove around but weren't able to locate them. I pressed charges for endangering our child. I knew it was a ploy, to cause me to worry about our son and to keep me from proceeding with the child support case.

He always knew how to play crazy when it suited him. When Shaquil was returned to me I asked him what had happened. He said him and his dad were hiding behind cars and finally climbed in a tree when they saw cops. He told me he was cold and scared.

I was so angry. I was scared for my son because his father only acted crazy with me, but was able to keep it together in front of authorities. But I was so quick to accept a bipolar diagnosis from overly eager doctors that did no real evaluation. I was afraid he'd get custody and of what my suicide attempt might look like to a court.

I knew I had to leave. I had no choice, but fear overwhelmed me. I began to pray to God, to ask him to take this situation and work it out. I felt like I needed not only to understand what Anthony had done to me, but what I had done to myself and my children. I asked God to reveal these things to me, so that I can truly repent. The only way I was going to overcome all the damage was if God worked on me. I was determined to do the real work it was going to take.

I could have focused on what Anthony had done but I wanted to know what had I done. I felt like I deserved this somehow, that I had done so much bad that I was getting paid back. I thought about Jake and that I didn't do the right things. I wanted to take responsibility for what I had done wrong. I have to say God started to reveal me to me and it wasn't pretty. First reveal was when I had to remember how I treated my mother, how I called her names.

I looked down on her and I carried so much anger for how my life turned out. I was struck by the realization that the very anger I had for my mom was the same anger my children would and could have for me. It was humbling, the discovery that I was no better, and maybe even worse. My mother had situations just as I had. She had a mother that didn't know her worth, who had been molested and violated. She had a husband that she allowed to mistreat her.

My mother continued the cycle, and as much as I thought it would never be me, it was me. I had almost taken my own life. I wasn't as strong as I thought I was. I was very weak.

I asked God for forgiveness and for the first time I didn't feel justified in my anger toward my mom. I felt ashamed that I had been so rebellious and disrespectful for so many years. This self-reveal was very hard because in every scenario I was a victim and now I was seeing for the first time my role in all of this, seeing all the choices that I had made. I wasn't only a victim but the villain. I continued to journal and pray and work through hurt and pain with honesty and sincerity.

I was having an encounter with God like never before. I was being prompted to repent for things I didn't even allow myself to think about. I remember so clearly hearing a voice that said, "You need to ask for forgiveness for murder." I thought about it. I just beat up people, I don't think anyone ever died. Then I remembered the abortion, the one I had no remorse about. I felt so bad because it wasn't until that moment that I realized that I had taken something that wasn't mine to take. I thought of the potential and a future that belonged to God. I quickly responded, "But God you know I could not have handled another child." And He said, "You could have handled anything if only you had trusted me with your life.

You only needed to trust me." I wept for my unborn child and asked for His forgiveness. I know I have done a lot of things Lord but I don't want to see anymore. I felt the heaviness of the disappointment that I had been. This would have to be a process. I asked for guidance as I resolved to do my very best to follow His instructions. I was done making excuses. The choice was obvious, I could give up or I could give in. I didn't know how or exactly what it meant, but I was ready to learn. Lord, I surrender. Teach me how!

CHAPTER 20

ACCOUNTABILITY AND PERSPECTIVE

FIRST LESSON IN SURRENDER IS ACCOUNT-ABILITY. I needed to accept responsibility for the mess I had made. The next step was to be remorseful and change my perspective. The third step was to repent and ask for forgiveness. This was very difficult because in order to see myself, I had to be very lenient on those that I believed hurt me. I had to take off my victim label.

I felt like a jerk when I really started to play back my life and see my actions. No, I wasn't to blame for all the bad that went wrong. I was safe to blame my molestation and my rape on my attackers, but even more so on the enemy's attacks against my life. I had to understand that in spite of what I was dealt I still had a choice. I had a choice to stay in school.

I had a choice to not rebel against the instruction of my mother. I had a choice to go out and have sex or not. I had a choice to not react in fear. My choice not to trust God had led me into relationships that could've taken me off of the path of my purpose. This last relationship could and should have destroyed me, but God protected me. There were clues in the beginning that it wasn't right. My anxiety about being able to provide for my children made me feel like my options were limited. I now know that that was a lie of the enemy and I never wanted to make that mistake again. I want to be led, I don't want to steer my own wheel against the Lord.

My heart was ready but my flesh was oh so weak. My own rationalizing would still get in the way of my ordered steps. The Lord wanted me to completely abandon the idea of returning to that home. So I went to my Aunt Tina, who managed apartments for lower income folks. The apartment wasn't in the best neighborhood, but neither the worst.

The up side was that it was walking distance from the community college I was attending. I could live there and go to school as long as I received Social Security. I could apply for financial aid and get my degree. I gasped for air when I saw the apartment; it was so small. I felt anxiety about how far I had slipped backwards. I envisioned Anthony and his parents living in that house, and remembered how I thought my mom was weak for not fighting for her home.

I decided I was not about to do what my mother did. She let William have the house while she moved into Aunt Tina's low-income housing in one of the worst neighborhoods in Baltimore. I was seeing history repeat itself and I was determined to disrupt that. I moved back into my house. I didn't know how I was going to get the lights in my name and get a judge to grant me complete and exclusive access to the home, but my kids needed to stay in their schools.

I phoned my dad to ask him to get me a two-ton truck so I could clean out the house. Months without lights had destroyed the fridge and I wanted to clean out all the garbage. I emptied out the upper floors then went into the basement and began throwing out anything that served no purpose. I got to underneath the steps and didn't expect much of anything but spider webs, but what I found was mildewed clothes—the ones that I would wash and then would mysteriously go missing. My outfits I laid out, my children's clothes, and all of my missing underwear were under the basement steps.

Anthony did all this to perpetuate my insecurities, and make me think I was losing my mind. This meant he had to sneak around the house, grab my clothes, and take them all the way to the basement. I would often catch him sneaking in when I left my car to my sister, or when he thought I was asleep he would slip past me, but this here took being a creep to another level.

By now I was convinced that Anthony was crazy. And I at that point I started to realize just how committed he was to trying to drive me crazy. It didn't make sense. What had I done to him that warranted such hate? I never tried to destroy him. Never falsely accused him. In fact, I usually tried to cover up his insanity, although mostly out of embarrassment. But still I did not set out to harm him. I heard the prompting of the Holy Spirit working with me. "I know you are frightened but you must let go of this home and trust Me." I returned to my Aunt Tina and signed the lease. I had to wait a week to get my next check to pay for a moving vehicle and I knew I would have to put a lot in storage, but I was ready. Or so I thought. The big day came when I received my keys and I took my kids to the apartment. I expected reservation but when my daughter walked in she looked so heartbroken, "This is so ugly and small, and I don't want to live here," she said. I instantly fell back to, "I can't fall this far back. Even before I got married I had a cute apartment in a nice county neighborhood."

This isn't fair, why should he get to keep the house? I felt like I had to start again from scratch after all that I put up with just to walk away empty handed, no job, worse than I was when I started. He planned to get me out, and he won. I made such a strong case that my fighter mode returned and I was right back at figuring out how to go back to that house.

In reality, it wasn't really about the house but I worried about what people would say. I was embarrassed and humiliated. The spirit of shame was the same spirit that kept me in this abusive, chaotic marriage. I can imagine how disappointing it had to be for my Heavenly Father to have to get me to let go again. I had my sister take me back to the house that I once shared with Anthony and evaluate what I was going to do.

I arrived at the home to find it empty. Everything I owned, my children's belongings, all gone. I had been moved out like trash. I believe Anthony saw I had cleaned out the house and because legally he couldn't get me out, he took everything I had to return to. Everything that was in that home I had replaced, it belonged to me and my children. The clothes, their toys, our beds, the furniture, all gone! I laid on the floor and sobbed. I needed a break. I know I'm not perfect Lord, but who deserves this! I had my sister Victoria call Anthony to ask where our belongings were. He said they were in storage. For the next several months Anthony would refuse to give me info on my belongings, and would only say they were in storage. I decided that I wouldn't call him anymore because he enjoyed hearing me grovel. I wouldn't give him the satisfaction.

After I finished crying and I stood up, I got this strength that was supernatural. I no longer cared what people thought. I was determined to get us back from this. I will not be destroyed or bitter; I will be better. I still thought that the apartments were too small so I looked in the paper and found a place that wasn't too much more and I went to look at it. I remember the apartments my Aunt Tina lived in when I was a teenager and I had gone to stay there with her when things got too bad at home.

The apartments were still not in the best neighborhood but at least it was spacious. I wasn't afraid of the area because I had lived in the hood before and I could handle myself. My children would have a longer commute but would stay in their old school. I realized what hadn't killed me was making me stronger. I took on a positive attitude and remembered it was a challenge and God was with me. Even though I had lost my furniture I hadn't lost myself. I was still the same woman that survived in Virginia, and I was more able and stronger. I went inside the office and the landlord who was from Israel told me he didn't do credit checks and I would have to come up with a deposit of one month's rent. I was taken down to see my apartment; it had burnt carpet and the walls that needed to be painted but I could see potential. They told me they needed a couple of weeks so I got a money order and gave them my deposit. My Aunt agreed to let me out of the lease.

Moving day was so easy since I had nothing to move in except the things that I had taken to my sister's: two garbage bags of clothes for me and my children and my computer. I was so happy that my computer was with me. My family gave me a TV.

I bought three air mattresses and I was ready. I went to the apartment and it looked exactly the same, no paint, and no removal of the carpet. I held on to my optimism and asked the landlord why it hadn't been done. He explained that he would take a hundred dollars off of my deposit and asked that I be patient while he has to get a new person to come in and do the work. He said, "I knew it was urgent for you to move in, so I figured you wouldn't mind rather than wait."

I decided I would be grateful; this was me turning over a new leaf. I spent the night in my apartment with a grateful heart. Rather than complain I chose to praise God for my home, to praise God for my mattresses, and to really praise God for his mercy. I wasn't just giving lip service, I truly was thankful because I knew that the plans for me by the enemy were to destroy me. I was free and I was able to be and do whatever I wanted. I praised Him day and night for freedom and a sound mind. I decided during my first few nights to go right to work and found a part-time job. I saw that Macy's was hiring in their shoe department and Christmas was right around the corner. I knew that I would also need a little more income to keep up with my monthly bills. I applied and was called in for an interview.

During my interview I was told that they had something else in mind for me. The manager took me down to the makeup counter and introduced me to the manager, Kim. She said, "She is beautiful, she will do well working behind the counter." I was to sell beauty products and if asked, to apply makeup. Most of the women there were trained by the company to put on makeup. Kim favored me because I possessed a natural ability to draw customers with my warmth. She said that she had plans to make me a supervisor and send me to be trained at their headquarters.

I was excited but really only wanted a part-time job. My plan was still to go to school. I liked that I was working and felt like I was getting back to being able to handle things. I was free from attacks, and I was able to think more clearly.

I needed a second opinion about my diagnosis as I was waiting on future court dates to dissolve my marriage. I looked up a reputable psychologist and found Dr. Hinson. On the day of my appointment I was given several evaluations. I had never been given a test at my other doctors' offices, they barely asked questions. This confirmed that my former doctor was getting his information from his patient, my husband. One of the tests I was given had 500 questions. I was asked questions about how I felt in different situations. I answered honestly. After the testing, Dr. Hinson asked me about my life and my experiences. He was patient. He didn't seem to have an attitude like my other doctor had. He concluded that I was not nor have ever been bipolar but was suffering from post-traumatic stress disorder, PTSD, which is defined as a disorder that may develop after a person is exposed to one or more traumatic events, such as major stress, sexual assault, terrorism, or other threats on a person's life. The results of the testing indicated signs of high levels of trauma comparable to that of prisoners of war. I now had a better understanding of what I was going through and was determined to heal properly.

I began looking for understanding by reading my Word. I took great comfort in Psalms. I had felt like I had been in a war and could feel the force of enemies seen and unseen. I held onto the belief that God would deal with my enemies and that I would be victorious, just as he did for David.

In my new apartment I felt like I could think clearly and I remembered somethings as I was preparing to go back to court. I still had an upcoming court date from when Anthony snatched Shaquil and ran. I mostly knew I needed to be prepared for our pending court dates for our divorce. I was so ready to move on. The first court date was just to schedule the next dates.

While we were before the judge, the clerk told us to state our addresses. I tried to tell the judge I had an upcoming domestic case and I didn't feel safe giving him my address. She didn't care and forced me to tell him my new address.

I did and Anthony laughed. It was funny to him that I had to move to such a bad neighborhood from where we once lived.

I made the most of my time in my new place. I remembered Anthony was accused of impregnating a woman by the name of Adana. She was the African woman I had spoken to on the phone. I tried to locate her on social media. I wasn't successful until I looked her up on a site that was exclusively for Africans. I found someone related to her and left a message.

Adana called me the next day. I reminded her of our previous conversation and told her that I was Anthony's soon-to-be ex-wife and wanted to help her get the support for her child. Even though he told me that it was not his child, I wanted to prove his infidelity. Adana was skeptical but she eventually told me where she was staying. Surprisingly, it was two blocks away on the same street where I was now living.

CHAPTER 21

WALKING BY FAITH

THIS WAS AMAZING! I lived right down the street from my husband's mistress at the same time I was preparing to go to court for a divorce. I just knew God wanted me to get a big alimony check. Adana told me she would come with one condition: that I bought her a 40 oz. bottle of beer.

I thought to myself, I will get you anything you want, and since I often drank wine to relax, it would be fine. I went down the street, not knowing what to expect. I was preparing myself to see this African princess as I had always imagined every woman he cheated with looked like. I told myself I was beautiful and to remember not to compare myself.

When I arrived at the house and I was about to ask the woman outside if she knew Adana. Before I did she said, "Are you Khalilah?" I said, "Yes." I knew by that thick accent that she was Adana. I was taken back because she was not only unattractive, she didn't even look like *anyone's* type. Her eyes were yellow and bulging and her skin was dehydrated and peeling and she looked like she was possibly homeless. Now I was so confused. My soon-to-be ex-husband was crazy, but how could he sleep with this woman? And have unprotected sex at that? I was now getting a better sense of how crazy this man really was.

Adana invited me into this small apartment that several people were occupying. The one thing that I saw that troubled me the most was this middle-aged man whose spirit oozed perversion. The way he looked at this little girl, a little girl who was the spitting image of Anthony, was disturbing. I couldn't believe this child looked more like Anthony than my own son. I became so protective I wanted to snatch her up and take her from this home. I took them back to my apartment so we could talk.

When we were back at my place, Adana kept staring at me. She said, "What in the world was he looking for?" She continued, "You are gorgeous, what was he thinking?" I didn't respond. I asked her about the relationship to see if they were serious. She told me they met in July 2005, the same month he tattooed my name on him to prove he was serious about not cheating. She became pregnant that October, the same month that he had me arrested for allegedly hitting him with a car.

She met him when she was a student in school studying computers; she was here on a student visa. She said he told her he lived with his baby's mother but they weren't together, he lets me stay there because I didn't have anywhere to go. He told her he loved her, gave her his nickname and a different last name. He never told her where he worked. When she wasn't able to get an abortion he just disappeared.

She said while they were together he would come in her home whenever he wanted and destroy her belongings. He destroyed her TV and would drag her around. I wanted to ask why did you let him do that but I heard myself before the words came out of my mouth.

I needed to remind myself of how Anthony abused me. She showed me a picture of her around the time that they met and she was attractive then.

How did she get here? Her visa had expired. She was bouncing from home to home with shady characters and she couldn't get out of bed without a drink. I knew that what she was going through was a direct result of dealing with Anthony and I felt so sad that she let herself go. While she was at my house I cooked some turkey wings. The more she talked the more she drank.

Once her beer was about gone, she changed. I gave her something to eat and the little Anthony look-alike reached up and asked her mother for some food and Adana balled up her fist and hit her as if she was an adult. I couldn't believe what I had just witnessed. I thought about beating her up but Anthony had made my reputation so bad that I didn't need another enemy.

I knew as the soon-to-be-ex-wife I couldn't be much help. I made a spilt-second decision and offered to let her stay with me. I would try to help her regain her self-respect and protect this little baby girl from abuse at the hands of her mother and the creep down the street. She accepted, happy to be getting the help she needed. It solved her problem.

She had only promised to pay rent down the street but never paid it. She knew she was about to be homeless again. I moved her in that day.

My heart was jumping because I don't know this girl and, as it is, I don't have anything but a computer and some air mattresses. But my concern for this 18-month-old baby girl had me throw reason out the window. It was as if my saving her would be a way of redeeming myself. Adana was an alcoholic who was so severely depressed that she needed me to sternly suggest baths. Her alcoholism was as bad as Anthony's mom's. I was no stranger to alcohol myself and would sometimes use it to self-medicate when I was anxious, but even at my worst I had nothing on Adana.

My landlord took an obsessive liking to me and offered me a job. Since he was creepy and would show up at my house with wine at 11 p.m. I decided I would be better off working at Macy's. When I looked across the alley in my neighbor's windows, I could see candles burning, because their lights were out. I was so curious because most everyone in the building besides me were on Section 8. I developed a civil relationship with one of the secretaries in the office. She would often tell me how much of a slumlord the landlord was.

He rigged all of the apartment lights so he had no bill, meanwhile the residents' electric bills would be six hundred and above each month when they should have ranged from fifty to a hundred dollars. He never did any real maintenance. He paid drug addicts from the neighborhood to rewire and patch up stuff. He never had any plans to replace my carpet or paint; he intended to say I did the damage and keep my deposit. I was so appalled because not only did the people renting his apartments have low incomes and were barely making it, he was having people lose their housing vouchers because they could not keep the lights on. I didn't know how I was going to do something but I was determined to.

I started making calls to Section 8. I was told that I needed to call the electric company to send out an investigator. I also went door to door and received signatures about what people were experiencing and informed the residents that they could put their rent in escrow until the landlord completed repairs in the apartments. Some listened, and I became a problem for my landlord.

When I returned home I would find that my drawers were ransacked. Pictures I had taken for my divorce, of how Anthony would destroy my belongings, would be sitting on the counter when I had put them in the drawer. I know it was reported to him that I took pictures of the horrible conditions in the building, so it appeared he was attempting to retrieve the photos. But I always kept them in my car. I drove myself and a few neighbors down to the courthouse to see about putting our rent in escrow until the repairs were completed. It was suggested that I apply for a townhome that was near my church. I assumed it would be a waste because if they did income verification no one would rent to me.

While I waited on the court date for my escrow case, I still had to appear in court for Anthony regarding the time he snatched Shaquil and ran. I was confident that when I showed up for court this time with his mistress and daughter he wouldn't be laughing. I walked in holding his beautiful look-alike, Adana came in behind me, I sat down and his daughter turned around and looked right at him, as if she knew who he was.

The case was postponed, but out in the hall his divorce attorney, who was also representing him in his criminal matter, said she would have him give me child support if I would let this be. I told her he needed to pay child support on his daughter as well. His lawyer said that wasn't her concern. The look on Anthony's face was priceless.

He tried to sneak only glances at his daughter, but when he couldn't help but see the resemblance he started to loosen his tie as if it suddenly got hot. I didn't need him to go to jail; I wanted him to be accountable. I did need support. Eventually I would reluctantly drop the charges and focus on our pending divorce. There was no way he had expected me to find his daughter's mother when he was so clever about keeping us apart. He hadn't bet on a supernatural God that was ordering my steps.

The miracles continued. I kept taking every concern to Wednesday night prayer meeting. No matter what it was, my prayers were being answered. I prayed harder the closer the court date of the escrow case got. If I was awarded escrow, I would still need to break my lease. I had tried getting a place an hour away so I could get away from Anthony but I had no rental history that I could use so I was denied. I was told by another person to try the townhomes near church, but I couldn't see how I could be approved. The day before I went to court I sat down at my computer and in my search engine was the name of the townhomes. I never typed that in, I knew it popping up was divine. I said okay Lord, I get the hint, I will go apply today. I talked to the assistant manager and explained my situation and told her what I made. She said even though I didn't qualify she was going to do everything to help me. She said it would be 3-5 business days to get a decision. I asked God, "Now what?" It was a Wednesday so I took it to the prayer meeting.

Pastor Rupert said that you should have an offering when you come into the house of God; all I had on me was my rent money that I had to take to court. When I left prayer meeting I was planning to stop and get a money order. I prayed and said, "Lord, all I have is my rent." I made a decision at that moment to do something I had never done before. I took a large portion of my rent and when the offering plate passed me I secretly dropped it in. I felt scared and excited at the same time. I said to God, "Now you have to do something." I went home and prepared for court.

The next morning I received a call from the townhome assistant manager. She said, "You're approved!" I couldn't believe it. She said it took 3-5 business days! She told me she convinced her manager to give me a shot. I was so excited but I still needed to show up in court without rent, and now wanting to break my lease. My other neighbors that I had brought with me to apply to put their rent in escrow had a court case the same da y .

I went in and showed the judge my photos and gave her my recordings of the inappropriate messages the landlord would leave on my answering service. She told him that my rent was abated and asked me what I wanted to do. I said I want to leave. She said, "When?" I told her in a week, the same time the townhome would be ready. She said, "Done!" And gave a strong warning to the landlord to leave me alone. He was so angry.

The other neighbors still had to put their rent in escrow but I knew I had just witnessed the power of God who moved and honored my radical faith. Miracles kept happening at Faith Church, when I relied on prayer.

CHAPTER 22

CURSE BREAKER

MY FAITH WAS GROWING. Looking at all I had overcome, I began to praise God but in praising God, I guess I could say I was also taunting the enemy. I started to yell, "You thought you were going to get my daughter! You had plans to get my daughter but you can't. Devil, you're a liar and you lose!" I was just a baby in spiritual understanding, and maybe should have stayed humble and continued on in the Holy Spirit training. And if I wasn't so preoccupied, I would have noticed the major changes in my daughter—her constant sobbing, clinginess and rage.

She wanted to stay up under me like a baby. I guess if I wasn't bent on trying to save Anthony's daughter maybe I would've seen that I needed to save my own. The changes I observed I attributed to having to move and readjust, to having less and leaving her friends behind. I expected her to come out of this place of despair and to be stronger and more resilient. I wasn't too worried about my daughter; after all, she was naturally confident, funny and brilliant.

She was that young woman that would give her allowance to feed the needy. Once, she slept outside with her camp to raise funds for the homeless. This was the same young woman who in elementary school protested against girls not being able to play football then was allowed to play.

Kacey always looked down on the promiscuous attention-seeking girls, the misguided ones. I admired her so much—she was nothing like me at her age. She wrote evocative poetry, and when I took college courses, even though she was only in the sixth grade, she would often help by doing my homework. And remember, I got all A's. My beautiful chocolate skinned butterfly, she would get her wings.

After all, she was my motivation to do better. I hated the disappointed look on her face and I was determined to regain her respect. In spite of all that I had exposed her to, she still persevered. "Baby Girl, I know it looks bleak but God won't leave us here, trust Him." I realize I relied on her more than I should have, more than a 14-year-old should be relied on. "Kacey feed the kids. Take them to school. Clean up," I'd say. Growing up I chose not to be a kid, then inadvertently kept my daughter from being one.

A year or two before our move, Kacey's father, Tyrone, was released from prison. He'd challenged his conviction in the courts, and it was decided that they lacked sufficient evidence to convict him. Kacey was excited to have her father in her life, and the bonus was that he had a younger daughter by another woman, so she could finally have a sister.

Upon his release, he continued the relationship with this young woman, whom he had a child with before going to prison. She had other children of the same age group.

Kacey was so excited to have sisters. In the beginning, I was very skeptical about allowing her to hang around them in my absence. So I would let them hang out at our house; but since that was no longer an option, Kacey would wear me down about going with them. I gave Tyrone the rule, "Don't let Kacey out of your sight." He agreed.

I knew I didn't really have a right to keep her from him. I would learn a couple of years later that I was right to be concerned. My daughter's drastic behavior change wasn't just about her having to adjust to a new home and new friends, but my child had been raped at 14.

One time while visiting her dad's house she was allowed to attend a neighborhood party with the other girls. At this party she was dragged out, away from the other teens, and raped. I can only guess why my daughter chose not to tell me, maybe because she feared I would blame her father and keep her from him. If so, her guess would have been right. I told Tyrone time and time again not to let her out of his sight. Even when she went to the movies with her friends, I was a chaperone. He gave me his word. I suspected that his feelings of guilt about not being there for Kacey for years probably caused him to let her get away with anything, even if that meant lying to me.

When I was still in the dark about the rape I prayed a lot. I was also especially stern, just as my grandmother had been with me. I would say, "Get up and get over it!" The "nobody owes you anything" approach was inappropriate but I didn't know about the rape. I needed to keep my focus. Operation "get back up and get your mind right" was in full effect. The first order of business was "stay positive." I was determined not to dwell on the past but to instead look forward to a brighter tomorrow; that was my action plan.

My girlfriend Alisha and I created vision boards. On my vision board there was a 2007 Nissan Maxima because at the time I had a 1996 version. I had a picture of a man and woman with the word "love" above them. I figured I'd start planning what my next marriage would look like.

Two pictures were of houses, one of a townhome and another of a big beautiful house. I figured the townhome would be my beginning, and the mansion is what I would lead up to. Many nights I slept on the air mattress in that horrible home in the worst neighborhood. I'd gaze at my vision board and believe with all my heart that life was going to get better. I stopped working for Macy's.

I found a pro bono lawyer service that sent me to an attorney who agreed to handle my divorce at no charge. His recommendation was that I not work while this process continues, since Anthony was obligated to continue financial support. When I retained my lawyer he sent Anthony several requests to release my belongings. In the beginning they were ignored but eventually just in time for moving, Anthony, his mother and father accompanied me to the storage that held most of my belongings. I discovered he had thrown away all of our clothes, even the children's. All of the children's toys, except Shaquil's automatic car minus the charger (which made it useless), were gone.

He, of course, took the big screen TV, most of the screws for my bed and my baseboard for my mattress. A lot of my belongings were broken. I decided to be grateful for what was returned. Adana was with me, and Anthony's mother tells her how beautiful she was. I knew the manipulation games had begun. During this transition, I heard clearly the still small voice of the Holy Spirit telling me this woman ought not to be allowed to move in to my new home with me.

My question to God was, "Where will she go?" And as always, God had already worked that out. Adana, who had grown tired of me monitoring her alcohol intake, found a place with so-called friends. I was still concerned for her daughter; and she didn't mind letting me keep her and visiting her from time to time. My new townhome looked amazing compared to where I had been.

The neighborhood seemed peaceful, but again that was in comparison. The most amazing part of my new home was that I was within walking distance from Faith Church. About this time my child support hearing had come up, so instead of the $462 that Anthony was originally ordered to pay the court decided he should pay $628. Right after that victory, disaster would strike again.

One night, as I was relaxing at home with Adana and Anthony's baby girl Tee-Tee, I received a call from Adana's roommate. "Please come get her, she is drunk and zapping out!" I put Tee-Tee in her car seat and sped down to get Adana before she was arrested. I was the only one that could calm her, the only person she'd listen to when she was intoxicated. As I headed straight down Pratt Street, a car was backing up from one side of the street to the other and I had a full on collision with this vehicle. Luckily, there was no harm to either me or the baby girl, but my car was totaled. I think the young lady with the car full of people was drunk, and she was set on going into the bar on the corner when she spotted a better parking space across the street. This was the worst thing that could happen at this time, when I was trying so hard to move forward. My insurance had lapsed, and I had no coverage.

The cop on the scene wasn't interested in doing any type of investigation, so she deemed us equally at fault. Are you kidding me? I was driving straight, and she reversed…and we're equally at fault? I remembered I was going to stay positive no matter what it looked like and trust God. So I calmly called a family member and said, "My car has been totaled. Will you please come get me?"

It was as if everything that I had with Anthony was being taken, but I realized that God was in control and if He was going to strip me down it was because He had every intention to build me back up. I also decided that I was not equipped to handle Adana's issues. Her addiction was way more than I had the energy for. I helped with her baby girl and that was it. Now I'm in my townhome with no vehicle, in a different part of town that I had never lived in, knowing absolutely nothing about the bus system.

The only place that I could get to was church. Having to stay in the house and do nothing day in and day out would make it so difficult to stay positive. I would frequently find myself getting so angry with Anthony that I would have to fight thoughts of seeing him hit by a truck. I know these thoughts weren't right, so I prayed, "Lord, if you don't help me forgive this man, my anger will destroy me and he would have won." I was so determined to get through this. "Lord if you say I'm supposed to forgive him, You have to show me how." The Holy Spirit told me that I had to pray for him. "Pray for what, the only thing that I desire for this man is that he dies."

What a patient and loving Father I serve, because He instructed me to pray for him to be a better father for and to Shaquil. The love I had for my son was greater than the hate I had for my soon-to-be ex-husband. It was still hard at times, I would have to stay on my knees it seemed for hours. Every time I felt enraged by the thought of what he had done to my children and me, I got on my knees and prayed for him.

Sometimes I had to pray that what I was praying, I meant. I would pray and pray. When I felt the anger subside, I'd get off my knees. At times the anger would return with a vengeance, and I would have to fall to my knees again. Being immobilized, with nothing but time and memories, I needed an outlet. A neighbor, who was just a few doors down, had spoken in passing but we never made conversation.

Her name was Trudy and out of the blue she knocks on my door and says, "This delivery company is hiring. I see you're not working and neither am I. I'm about to go down there and see if they have any positions available for me. You want to come?" I was about to say no but I felt a nudge from the Holy Spirit to go. What could it hurt? I know my lawyer said not to get a job but I heard this is a good company, so I went. There were no customer service, secretary or even receptionist positions available. What they were hiring for was all labor and they were only part-time. The positions started at $8.50 an hour.

Trudy was ready to go. She had her CDL license. Just as we were about to leave the HR representative said the opportunity for promotion was great. Their delivery drivers made $75,000 a year. It took the average person approximately 3-5 years to get to that level but there are raises that happen in between. I never knew they made that much money, and with their union contracts being revised every five years workers continue to receive raises. I was sold!

Yes, I did want to become a nurse but the reality was that given how much time I had spent away from school, that when I did resume college the math and biology would be huge challenges. The thought of doing physical work thrilled me, and I knew I was strong enough to do it. The fact that only seven women in the building, out of a hundred men were drivers, didn't at all intimidate me. If I had overcome Anthony, I just knew I was tough enough.

We had to come back for an interview. During my interview the hiring supervisor told me that even though I had no warehouse experience there was something about me that told him I would do an amazing job.

He asked me where I saw myself with the company in the next five years and I said, "I will be a driver." I was hired on the spot. Unfortunately, even with her warehouse experience and CDL license my neighbor did not get the job. This job represented a way out. Now I was confident that I was on the path of being able to provide for my children. It meant never having to rely on anyone else to provide a safe home.

When I began to work, I worked so hard that managers and supervisors took notice. My job was to unload tractor trailers. It didn't matter, I had joy and I couldn't easily be moved. Some asked, why I smiled so much. I sang often a song entitled "Grateful", because I knew what had been done for me.

About 2 months into working, my divorce date came up. My divorce attorney had advised me not get a job, but I didn't make very much anyway. I came in and I prayed "Lord have your way". We went in and I no longer cared about the house or even showing his infidelity, or exposing the child he tried to escape from caring for. It was a peace that came on me that was unexplainable. I felt so relaxed, as if God was breathing on me. The need I once had to tell what I went through disappeared, I just wanted to get a divorce. I didn't even care about the alimony I was due, I just wanted it to be over. Anthony started with his lies, saying that he paid for everything, because he had stolen all my receipts, when I replaced everything in the house. I knew that I could prove it because I paid with my debit card and the receipts reflected it, but instead of proving he lied, I just said ok.

At that moment the only thing I cared about was getting my life back. I walked out feeling just as nervous but excited as I did when I put my rent in the offering basket. I didn't know how or what but I knew God was shifting it all around for my good. One Wednesday night on my way to prayer meeting I started to think about all that had transpired in my life, the realization that I had been under a curse and so had my mom and grandma. My desire was that my daughter would not have to experience a man like Anthony, and my sons would not become him.

That prayer meeting, when a call for prayer requests was made, I raised my hand. When I was given the microphone I told my church that I believed my family and I were under a generational curse and I wanted them to pray that that curse would be broken. Our new associate pastor, who I had never formally met, Pastor Green, leaned over to me and whispered in my ear, "God told me that you would be the one in your family who was going to break this curse." Then the elders gathered around me and laid hands on me and prayed for me.

Though in the past I have experienced immediate breakthroughs when I brought my burdens and concerns to prayer meeting, this time relief would not be instantaneous nor would it be simple. Little did I know I was only on the basic level of spiritual warfare training and that those persistent demons that kept showing up from generation to generation were not going to give up so easily.

God would get all the glory. My praise became even more intense. Thanking God for another day meant so much more because at one point I wanted to die. Praising God for my health could not be contained because I knew the devil tried to make me lose my mind. My God was teaching me to let go and trust him no matter what and my pain had purpose.

God loved me even though I was yet still in the world, my steps were being ordered. He was meeting me right where I was. All I really wanted was for God to give me a good job, so I could take care of my children and buy a nice home and car. His plans were so much higher.

The process that I went through was not just about me. The most amazing thing was that He didn't wait for me to get it all together. He focused on healing me from the inside, and as I surrendered, the more I changed. I was like David being prepared for my Goliath. My eyes were opened, I knew I could no longer keep fighting in the flesh, but I was waging a spiritual battle. I was in preparation season and being readied for the fight of my life. Everything I experienced and survived would be preparing me to be everything that I was always destined to be.

I want to encourage you that no matter what obstacles you face, our Father loves you. He has a plan for you, give Him your brokenness. He isn't looking for perfection but a surrendered will. He doesn't need you to have it all together first, those rules come from man, He doesn't want to punish you either. He wants to love you back to Him. The adversities will come but they come to make us stronger. Know that God is the beginner and finisher of our faith.

There would be many more battles ahead of me, but my confidence was in knowing that I would not be facing them alone. Every way that the enemy attacked me, was an indication of my calling. I stand in truth, giving a voice to the silent secrets that have kept so many in chains. I declare that by the blood of Jesus we are set free! The greatest part of this story has yet to be told.

To be continued...

Acknowledgements

First and foremost, I wish to give all the glory to my Lord and Savior Jesus Christ, in whom, I am redeemed, renewed and set free.

I want to thank my amazing, selfless and loving husband Michael Johnson. I could not have walked this path of healing without you by my side. I know that God put us together. With you I have experienced what it means to be loved to life. You are my friend, lover and a reflection of Gods unconditional love for me. Thank you for always seeing me.

I want to thank my Mother, My Grandmother and all of the women of this family that have taught me great lessons. My Mother in-law Jessie Mae, My Granddad, my Dad, and Step-Dad Barry.

I want to acknowledge my sons Devonta, Kobe, My daughter Kaira, and my grandbabies Aleah, Amauri and Khalil. Walk in your freedom!

My Sisters, Brothers, Brother In-law, Nieces, nephews, and all of my family.

I want to thank Pastor E.T. Stoddard . You have mentored, encouraged and taught me so much. You have always seen in me what I could not see in myself. I thank you greatly for your words of affirmation and time invested in my growth.

A special thank you to Pastor James Black Sr. who challenged me to write this book. I thank you for your obedience, wisdom and mentorship.
My Miracle City Church Family, and Pastor David Franklin and Wife Cynthia Franklin.

I want to also thank my friend and Web /Cover designer, Darren Cumberbatch of Awesome Ministry. You are a talented brother. I appreciate you going above and beyond the call and being a stand up dude. You are a friend until the end.
I want to thank my editor Debora M. Ricks for helping me see this project through.

To all of my prayer warriors that have prayed me through. Suze N., Valerie a.k.a. Lady, Renee, Pastor Chenay W., Shervon B., Cherraine M., Angel K., Natasha B., Elder Dexter R.& Renita R., Elder Gary J., Elder Denise J., Elder Tabitha H., Elder Howard, both Elder Hatchers, Donny Smith, Mike&Leanore J., Leonard M., Deacon Swann, All of the Deacons, Leanne M., Alvienia B., Monique D., Marlon B., Tanya C., Davesus O., Trinity C., Prayer warrior team. My Sabbath School class, and Sheri H.

Made in the USA
Middletown, DE
21 January 2016